Henry Clay Fish

Harry's Conflicts

Life Sketches

Henry Clay Fish

Harry's Conflicts
Life Sketches

ISBN/EAN: 9783337117382

Printed in Europe, USA, Canada, Australia, Japan

Cover: Foto ©ninafisch / pixelio.de

More available books at **www.hansebooks.com**

LIFE SKETCHES.

BY

HENRY C. FISH, D.D.

PHILADELPHIA:
THE BIBLE AND PUBLICATION SOCIETY,
530 Arch Street.

TO THE

YOUTH OF MY CONGREGATION,

AND TO

THE SUNDAY-SCHOOLS OF AMERICA,

THIS VOLUME

IS LOVINGLY INSCRIBED

BY THE AUTHOR.

CONTENTS.

I.
HARDNESS ENDURED... PAGE 7

II.
ERRORS ENCOUNTERED......................... 34

III.
CONTACT WITH THE WORLD...................................... 85

IV.
SAYING "NO".. 112

V.
HIGH AIMS.. 141

VI.
THE INNER NEED.. 176

VII.
NOW........ 205

Harry's Conflicts.

I.

HARDNESS ENDURED.

> "——Life is not as idle ore,
> But iron dug from central gloom,
> And heated hot with burning fears,
> And dipped in baths of hissing tears,
> And battered by the shocks of doom,
> To shape and use."

THE most critical period of human existence is that which falls between fourteen and twenty years of age. It is such because the character, to a greater extent than during any other equal term of years, then takes its unchanging type, its abiding form. Prior to this, the waxen tablet receives impressions more readily, but they are more readily effaced; subsequently thereto, the impressions received are comparatively few. In the one case the melted wax is too soft, and marks upon its watery surface are easily lost. In the other, it is too indurated to take the mould with readiness. During *this* period it is in the expanding, formative, transition state; and whether it be virtue or impiety that would leave its impress there, neither will again see so favorable a time for success.

Luther used to say that he was known in three places—heaven, earth, and hell. It is not too much to say that this is true of every youth during the period of which we speak. Heaven looks with interest upon this precious immortal. Society, religion, business, pleasure,—all turn the eye particularly to youth at this age, and would win them to their cause; while the enemy of all good at no other time is so diligent in plying his devices for their ruin.

We introduce Harry as a youth representing this class. Born in humble circumstances, like most of the boys of New England, we find him from the first inured to hardness, and tussling with all those inconveniences and hindrances incident to such a condition. One of a large family of children, and his father a "poor preacher," he learns the lesson of the closest economy, and does his part by working with his hands toward the common livelihood.

From the public school he enters the academy in "the middle of the town," and arises at four in the morning to get his lessons, that he may have time to "earn his board" before and after study and recitation hours. During the vacations he works upon the farm to recruit his finances. Scarcely of suitable age to assume such responsibilities, he hires himself out to keep a winter school, and "boards around," because he must, and because there were certain experiences necessary for him in that position.

With a natural distaste for farming, amounting almost to repugnance, and an unquenchable thirst for learning, he begs of his father the privilege of a liberal education, but receives the answer, "Glad as I would be to give you such advantages, I cannot afford it." "Then, can you give me my *time*, that I may educate myself?" modestly inquired Harry.

That was a great moment in his experience when his father answered him thus, as they were riding along in the wagon one Sunday on the way to church:

"My son, I believe God has given you a new

heart, and a desire to be useful in the world; if it is any advantage to you, I will give you the three years before you are twenty-one."

Harry's spirit leaped for joy. It was all he wanted; and he quickly replied,

"That is all I ask, father, for I know you could not do more; and now I set out to finish my education, and *I know I shall do it.*"

It was a long and rough road which Harry had to travel in reaching the goal of his youthful aspiration. Eight years later, however—years whose struggles we shall not depict—he stood in the hall of a theological seminary, which he was now about to leave, and made this remark: "The point of my fond hope is at last reached: I have fought my way through, by God's help, and completed my course of study; and I have done it without the assistance of any man or any society; and if I were to do it over again, I would follow the same way."

Is not this feature of *Harry's struggles* worth the consideration of the young? Among other charges of the apostle Paul to his son Timothy, he enjoined that he should "*endure hardness.*" This seems to be, in all things, a condition of success.

A French writer has said that "miracles are born of obstacles." And it was a remark of the eloquent Burke, that "difficulty is a severe instructor set over us by the supreme ordinance of a parental Guardian and Legislator, who knows us better than we know ourselves, as he loves us better too." We everywhere see that God is acting on this principle.

Hardship is the forerunner of excellence, the vestibule of greatness. The suffering, dying oyster yields the costly pearl. The smitten and wrenched tree, whose breast has caught for scores of years the autumn's wind and the winter's blast, bending, twisting, twirling, straining its twigs, boughs, and trunk, nurses and shoots down fartherest its roots and rootlets, grasping out everywhere in the sustaining soil, and sees, for its reward, the funerals of whole generations of saplings and plants that grew up without a fraction of this struggle. The finest alabaster is found on the stormiest coast. The patient, pale, plodding student unlocks the labyrinths of science. The climber up the rugged steeps, the adventurer into gulches and hazardous paths, tears up the clumps concealing ore, and strikes upon the placers where are the richest mines in the world's wealth. The bravest, hardiest, truest soldier comes to rank in the army. The slayer of the lion, of old, found the honey in his carcass. The chosen of the Lord were to suck honey out of the rock, and oil out of the flinty rock.

To look at some particulars, see how nations grow. It is always by rude processes. First, there are physical conflicts with forests and unsubdued soils and quarrelsome neighbors. Getting root, there come civic and commercial and political conflicts; and after these, induced upon a still higher civilization, there comes the conflict of ideas and discussion. Out of painful birth-throes nations are born. That ideal development of a race in happy conditions, where men easily and naturally work their way up into higher spheres, is all a phantasm. A race never has advanced, and never will advance, except by trying ordeals and painful processes. The history of the world shows it.

You may divide the past centuries into epochs, and write concerning them, as of the original epochs of creation, "And the *evening* and the morning were the (new) day." They will be seen to be made up of periods of darkness and of light—the *darkness*, however, always going before and *preparing for the light*. The history of man really begins in his apostasy.

It was but a gleam of sunshine that fell on his forehead in paradise, when he was enveloped in the darkness and blindness of sin, the emerging from which really makes up his history. At this low point, after the fall, in the gulf of deep distress, the social life of man began to improve, and it has been making steady advances ever since.

It was in the valley of trouble that the Messiah was first revealed. From that time forward, whenever darkness came on, it was but the beginning of a new day, and each new day, like those in Genesis, was in advance of the day that preceded it. The night was the period of gestation, of preparation. Forms of civilization decayed in long succession, but each worn-out form carried in its bosom elements which gave birth to a new and more perfect form. Great and mighty institutions gave way either to time or revolution or foreign invasion, but the germs of a new life were always existing in each decaying institution, and the period of decline for one people or age was a period of purifying process or preparation for that age or people that should succeed it.

Thus Central India, the earliest of historical nations, began in obscurity, reached a high position, then declined. But even this our age is enriched by its language and many elements of its philosophy. Egypt emerged from darkness into light, and then its sun set; but not until it had thrust forward into the Judaic and other nations its real acquisitions, there to receive a higher development. The same may be said of Assyria, and each of the old Eastern nations. So of Greece and Rome in the West. From small beginnings, and through innumerable difficulties, they forced their way up to greatness; but though their philosophy and theology had in them the seeds of death, and so decayed, yet how greatly, through their laws, and literature, and arts, have they contributed to prepare the world for its present condition!

In how low a vale of trouble, too, did the Israelitish nation begin its career—in the bondage of Egypt, and in the discipline of the wilderness!

Reference might also be made to the old ancestral peoples of Europe, from whom we and the several powerful nations have sprung.

How true this was, also, of the immediate founders of this republic, we all well know. They too passed through the Red Sea of suffering and the desert of trial, and then, and not before, came into their Canaan. So it has been all along the track of time. There is not a nation now advanced in the world's civilization that has not won its place by long years of severe and perhaps terrific effort.

The same is true of the religious progress of the world. The wickedness of the antediluvians waxed great, and they were cut off, but the flood became a benefit, a God-fearing people springing up in the land. The cities of the plain rioted in sensuality, and they were burned up, but their destruction arrested the general decay. The wars and tumults of Samuel's and David's time ushered in the meridian splendor of Solomon's reign. The rending of Israel into two parts hastened the extermination of idolatry. How terrible the night in which the old dispensation closed! no voice of prophet breaking its gloom for four hundred years, and but here and there one "waiting for the consolation of Israel." Upon that night arose the star of Bethlehem.

And a little later what do we see? The heaviest of troubles gathering upon the infant church. Peter denies his Lord. Judas betrays him. The disciples are bewildered and scattered, as sheep without a shepherd, for the sword has smitten that Shepherd, and he is now dead and buried. What blackness of darkness! Not a streak of day! But again what do we see? The clayey seals of the tomb cracking and crumbling asunder. The stone receding. The Sleeper awaking. The news spreading. The enemies confounded. The Messiahship admitted. The Saviour going up in clouds. The Holy Spirit coming down in torrents of power. Banners of the cross unfurled. The nations permeated with the gospel.

Remember, too, how Zion languished in the Middle Ages, and how this depression was succeeded by the glorious Reformation — strong from the attempts made to strangle it.

Observe in all this how true it is that adversities, trials, and troubles usually precede and prepare the way for the richest experience of the divine goodness; not because these depressions in themselves originate the better state —for this they could not do—but because God overrules evils and out of them educes good, and because vigor is the child only of struggle.

> " Not first the bright, and after that the dark;
> But first the dark, and after that the bright:
> First the thick cloud, and then the rainbow's arc;
> First the dark grave, and then the resurrection light.
>
> "'Tis first the night—stern night of storm and war,
> Long night of heavy clouds and veilèd skies;
> Then the fair sparkle of the morning star,
> That bids the saint awake and day arise."

From nations turn to individuals. Consider man, first, in a *religious* aspect, and observe that here he *must* struggle and contend in order to success. If you take a little child and analyze his moral composition, you will find that there are two principles, or dispositions, or natures, in him—the good and the evil—and these are adverse one to the other; so that, in growing up, the child is propelled by these inward forces in two different directions—conscience, or the better nature, urging toward the pure and the true and the good, but certain passions, desires, impulses, impelling him toward the low, the vicious, the debasing. This is always the case. Here there is, of necessity, a *collision*, a *wrestling;* for unless resistance to the lower impulse is perpetually made, the whole being is undermined and destroyed.

Besides, upon this susceptible human nature there is acting the unfriendly influence of bad examples and of bad customs, and bad habits and maxims prevailing among men, and also of numerous direct temptations, appealing constantly to his appetites and passions. Here, too, resistance is to be made.

Still more influential is malign *angelic power* ever acting upon man. "We wrestle against principalities, against powers, against the rulers of the darkness of this world, against spiritual wickedness in high places," says Paul. By these expressions undoubtedly are meant different ranks of malignant spiritual beings, unseen, but always operating upon us. Here, too, resistance is to be made.

The Scriptures designate these three evil forces now named, impelling us in the wrong direction, as "the *world,* the *flesh,* and the *devil.*" And if the better nature, animated by God's Spirit, is to get and hold the supremacy, how fierce and persistent will be the conflict! It is the whole animal nature, reinforced by corrupt society, and by subtle, powerful and myriad spirit-foes, operating against a single soul.

Then look at the intellectual part of our nature, and the character generally. Water, deprived of heat, cracks the basin. Powder, deprived of space and ignited, bursts the rock, but, burnt in the open air, is harmless. Nature wants room; but if it has room and scope, it takes things quietly. Shut it up, hedge it in, and it will take room; and by this it gets force. So character wants scope, and if it gets it readily is satisfied; but if it has to make room for itself, look out for results! For so has it gathered motive power.

Some writer has presented an ideal man who has reached mature age without having had to encounter a struggle with any antagonistic force, either natural or spiritual; who has had no desire but what has been gratified without any painful effort on his part; who has always done right because he had no motive to do otherwise; who has suffered nothing from pain, or sickness, or bereavements, or sympathetic grief,—in a word, one whose life has not been a warfare, but who has been wafted gently and peacefully down the stream of time, doing neither good nor evil.

Such a man, the writer maintains, could not be a Christian, because he has neither performed nor suffered the conditions essential to that character. He could not be called a good man, for his moral qualities have not been tested. He is a mere negative; there is nothing positive about him. From all that has yet transpired, we could form no opinion as to how he would act in the great battle of life. He might put forth qualities of moral heroism that would give him a high place among the great and good, the faithful and true; or he might be swept to perdition by the first blast of temptation or trial that assailed him. This is altogether a just view, and it shows the absolute necessity of antagonism in the development of character.

It is for the reasons above stated that those who are born and bred in affluence are so seldom possessed of strong and influential characters. Ease prevented future energy and power. If we are to expect the unsightly husk before the tempting kernel, the sprouting acorn before the giant oak, effort before strength, struggle before achievement, pain before pleasure, the law before the gospel, then we must not be surprised at the lack of stamina in any one who has never known want and difficulty.

Take the men of mark in any age. Were they rocked in the cradle of indulgence? Were they dandled in the lap of luxury? Anything else! They were sharp, stern, hardy, lordly men of iron muscle and adamantine faith, because they had been subjected to fierce antagonisms; because they had been nerved by use; because they had laid down in the furnace and been tested and refined and tempered in fiery ordeals. So was the stuff of men wrought into them.

There is a story told in ancient Roman mythology of Antæus, the son of Earth, who, in wrestling with Hercules, well nigh overcame that mightiest of wrestlers, because every time Hercules threw him on the ground he drew up into himself out of the ground a fresh invoice of strength, so that Hercules only killed him at length by lifting him aloft in the air and crushing him there between his iron arms. So do those forced into fierce conflicts, and sometimes thrown to the ground, get tenacity, toughness, tension, thereby. The Messiah, even, was made perfect (as a sympathizing one) through suffering. The twining, pliant, dove-like Simon is turned into the rocky *Peter* by the shocks and assaults of the adversary. The monk of Wittenberg towers into new boldness, and shoots higher "the rocket of his testimony," from being buffeted so fiercely by Satan and the pope, and driven up from earthly dependencies.

And in our day the poor laborer's son who, at seven years of age, axe in hand, is set to work to help to clear up a farm in a western forest; who gets in his whole youth not over a year's schooling; who goes, at nineteen, to New Orleans as a hired hand on a flat-boat, and coming back splits the rails for a log cabin and for a fence enclosing ten acres of land, and next year hires himself out at twelve dollars a month; and who is soon fighting for his country in the Black Hawk war, and is elected captain, and continues service in military frontier life; who afterward, as a postmaster, begins the study of law, borrowing books to do it with, and studying by the light of his evening fire, and so through difficulties struggles his way up, — *this* is the boy, the man, who has been styled "the second father of his country."

John Brown, afterward of Haddington, acquired his learning by dint of unwearied application, and in great poverty and discouragement. As a shepherd-boy he studied the Greek grammar till he mastered its principles. A very pleasant story is told of the way in which he obtained his first Greek Testament. He had now acquired so much of Greek as encouraged him to hope he might at length be prepared to reap the highest reward which classical learning could confer on him—the capacity of reading in the original tongue the blessed New Testament of our Lord and Saviour. Full of this hope, he became anxious to possess a copy of this invaluable volume. One night, having committed the charge of his sheep to a companion, he set out on a midnight journey to St. Andrews, a distance of twenty-four miles. He reached his destination in the morning, and went to the bookseller's shop, asking for a copy of the Greek New Testament. Some of the professors coming into the shop questioned the lad about his employment and studies. After hearing the tale, one of them desired the bookseller to bring the volume. He did so, and drawing it down, said,

"Boy, read this, and you shall have it for nothing."

The boy did so, acquitted himself to the admiration of his judges, and carried off his Testament, and when the evening arrived was studying it in the midst of his flock on the braes of Abernethy.

Dr. Livingstone, the famous African explorer, began life as a poor factory-boy. When but ten years of age, he was obliged to go to the factory at six in the morning, and remain until eight in the evening, with only brief intervals for breakfast and dinner. The hours from eight to ten he passed in an evening school, and not unfrequently his studies were continued until midnight. By this continued application, at the age of sixteen he had become a good Latin scholar. Scientific works and books of travel were his peculiar delight. "My reading," he says, "while at work, was carried on by placing my book on a portion of the spinning-jenny, so that I could catch sentence after sentence at my work. I thus kept up a pretty constant study, undisturbed by the roar of machinery." Thus he rose.

Dr. John Kitto, the eminent biblical scholar, when fifteen years old, was sent, a poor, deaf boy, to the workhouse, because his parents were

Harry's Conflicts.

Page 25.

unable to provide for him. Afterward he was apprenticed to a cruel and unreasonable master, who often required him to work from sixteen to eighteen hours out of the twenty-four. But under all of these disadvantageous circumstances young Kitto found time for the pursuit of knowledge. Every leisure moment was devoted to mental improvement. When his circumstances in life were more comfortable, he did not at all relax his industry. Of this he writes: "I cannot accuse myself of having wasted or misemployed a moment of my time since I left the workhouse." This wise improvement of his leisure moments laid the foundation of his great usefulness and world-wide fame.

Roger Sherman, at an early age, was apprenticed to a shoemaker. He was accustomed to sit at his work with his book before him, devoting to study every moment that his eyes could be spared from the occupation in which he was engaged. In this way he acquired his knowledge of mathematics, so that before he was twenty-one he was able to make astronomical calculations for an almanac published in New York. It was by such indefatigable industry that he attained an acquaintance with general science, logic, geography, history, philosophy, geology, and especially with law and politics.

Socrates, in early life, was entirely destitute of property, and once might have been heard saying in an assembly of friends, "If I had money I should buy me a cloak."

Mr. Crabbe, of Maryland, once said to a young friend, "You will have a large fortune, and I am sorry for it, as it will be the spoiling of a good lawyer. You may take," says he, "the whole population of the State, and select from it the fifty men who are most distinguished for talents, or any description of public usefulness, and I will answer for it they are all, every one of them, men who began in the world without a dollar."

One of our strongest and best men, a member of a late Presidential Cabinet, remarked concerning a former president of the college in Vermont where he graduated: "I never heard him utter what seemed to me a harsh reproof but once, and that was when he directed me never to appear again in the recitation-room without shoes. The harshness of the remark came from the fact that I had no shoes. I procured some, however, and, for the sake of economy, carried them in my hand to the door of the recitation-room, and then put them on." From extreme poverty he rose to honor, where he stood not "before mean men."

Powers, the celebrated sculptor, once said, when speaking of the expense of supporting his family, "To tell the truth, however, family and poverty have done more to support me than I have to support them. They have compelled me to make exertions that I hardly thought myself capable of; and often, when on the eve of despairing, they have forced me, like a coward in a corner, to fight like a hero."

Franklin, and Jefferson, and Webster, and others, might also be instanced in our country's history; but it is needless. The same has been found true in other countries. Columbus was a weaver; Sixtus V. was employed in herding swine; Æsop was a slave; Hogarth an engraver on pewter pots; Ben Jonson was a bricklayer; Akenside was the son of a butcher, so was Wolsey; Halley was the son of a soap-boiler; Belzoni the son of a barber; Blackstone and Southey were the sons of linen-drapers; Crabbe a fisherman's son; Keats the son of a livery-stable keeper; Captain Cook began his career as a cabin-boy. Luther might have been once heard, morning after morning, passing through the streets of the city where he then lived, singing his familiar songs to procure a few pennies or a loaf of bread. Bowditch studied mathematics on shipboard in hours snatched from service.

Ferguson first studied astronomy while tending sheep in Scotland, lying on his back and mapping out the heavens by means of a string with beads upon it. Arkwright was a barber till thirty years of age, and Burritt, in our own New England, who can read fifty languages, was an apprenticed blacksmith, at which business he worked as he studied. Goldsmith was once so pressed for means, when in college, that he sold out all his books to pay expenses, and wandered about for days, half alive and half starved, upon his last shilling. Long afterward, a merry tune upon his flute was his resort to procure a supper and night's lodging. He now lies in the poet's corner in Westminster Abbey. John Foster labored to procure knowledge, and became eminent under the most depressing circumstances. He was not able to meet his expenses at an insignificant academy but by laboring at his trade much of his time, and even then on the most niggardly scale.

Multitudes of other cases might be mentioned. As has been remarked, it is the old lesson, voiceful from every life that has a moral in it—from Bernard Palissy, selling his clothes and tearing up his floor to add fuel to the furnace, and wearying his wife and amusing his neighbors with dreams of his white enamel, through the unremunerative years; from Warren Hastings, lying at seven years old upon the rivulet's bank and vowing inwardly that he would regain his patrimonial property and dwell in his ancestral halls, and that there should be again a Hastings of Daylesford; from William Carey, hunting after the moral conquest of India, whether as he sat at the lap-stone of his early craft, or wielded the ferule in the village school, or lectured the village elders when the Lord's Day dawned,—it is the old lesson, a worthy purpose, patient energy for its accomplishment and a resoluteness that is undaunted by difficulties never so great. Thus have the great struggled up.

I have said thus much, my young friend, as a cheer to you if one of the strugglers. Very many of my readers, I know, will be obliged to follow the career of Harry in coming up to soundness of character and breadth of ability. But whatever obstacles present themselves, grapple with them in the unfaltering determination to deserve success. Compel your hindrances to become the architects of your greatness. It is only determined men that succeed to-day. Says a vigorous contemporary: "The genius of our social institutions is *movement.* The name of Washington is not enough to give popularity to his descendants, unless they have something of the nobleness, the head, the heart, of Washington. The wheel turns, but it is only stupidity and incapacity which fall to the bottom. Biographies of great men have but one commencement—'Born of poor but honest parents.'"

If you fail once, try again, in the spirit of the eminent D'Israeli, who, when he broke down in his first speech in the British Parliament and took his seat amid contemptuous jeers and laughter, pluckily called out, "I will sit down now, but the time is coming when you *shall* hear me." That was a prophecy. They did hear him, at length, and own him as a leader, too.

Bear in mind that no struggle is too dear a

price to pay for real, genuine eminence in any honest calling.

> " Better to stem with heart and hand
>   The warring tide of life, than lie
> Unmindful, on its flowery strand,
>   Of God's occasions drifting by :
> Better with naked nerve to bear
> The needles of this goading air
> Than in the lap of sensual ease forego
> The godlike power to do, the godlike aim to know."

I hope, dear reader, that you are a Christian. If so, accept the one condition here presented upon which you are to become an *eminent* Christian.

In the language of the quaint Trapp, Think not to find God in the gardens of Egypt, when Moses found him not but in the bush. Many love Canaan but for the wilderness; commend the country, but look upon the conquest as impossible; would sit in the seat of honor with Zebedee's children, but will not drink the cup of affliction. No wearing the crown but by bearing the cross first. Christ himself was not glorified till first crucified.

The religion of this day is undoubtedly too easy. It is too soft and effeminate. *Wrestling* needs to be done now, as of old. The Christian conflict is no dream; it is a reality. Every one is against us, except One. Ours, then, *must be* no languid, dreamy, delicious religion, lying still to rest, but a religion of activity, of enterprise, of sanctified ambition—a religion which wears armor, which wields weapons, which points onward to a crown. Aim at such a religion as this. If you are not a Christian, still keep in mind the motto, " No cross, no crown." If piety costs something, the *lack* of it costs more.

If not a Christian, two motives ought to influence you at once to become a true follower of Christ. One is the glorious end of the fight of faith. A French officer who was a prisoner on parole at Reading met with a Bible. He read it, and was so struck with its contents that he was convinced of the folly of skeptical principles and the truth of Christianity, and resolved to become a Protestant. When his gay associates rallied him for taking so serious a turn, he said, in vindication, "I have done no more than my old school-fellow, Bernadotte, who is become a Lutheran."

" Yes, he became so to obtain a crown."

"My motive," said the Christian officer, "is the same; we only differ as to the *place*. The object of Bernadotte is to obtain a crown in *Sweden;* mine is to obtain a crown in *heaven*." Is not the crown of eternal life worth striving for?

The other motive I refer to is that of loyalty to Christ your King. During the late war a color sergeant, while holding the flag, had been shot through the head and instantly killed. The flag was then seized by another. No sooner had he raised it than he too was shot, the ball severing his jugular vein. When he fell, young Chandler, a corporal of Co. F, 44th N. Y. Regiment, who had been wounded in the leg and arm, with his wounds bleeding, crept to the staff, and with great effort raised it the third time. In a moment he was shot in the breast and also fell. After lingering a few days in intense agony, death came to his relief. His last words were: "I regret that I have only one life to give to my country!" Oh, in the service of One deserving so much of you as does the blessed Jesus, ought you not to be willing to go even unto death, and then to regret that you had only one life to give to such a Saviour?

II.

ERRORS ENCOUNTERED.

"Oh how this tyrant, Doubt, torments my breast!
My thoughts, like birds which, frightened from their nest,
Around the place where all was hushed before,
Flutter and hardly nestle any more."

HARRY experienced religion and united with the church when about seventeen years of age. For a while his enjoyment was sweet and uninterrupted. But like too many, he gradually became less careful as to secret prayer, Scripture reading, the observance of the Lord's Day, and attendance upon the means of grace; so he fell into a season of darkness, and was assailed by doubts upon almost every point of the gospel faith.

His inquiring turn of mind, no doubt, had something to do with this. It is not true, as is sometimes asserted, that the keenest intellects are apt to be skeptical. Knowledge is the friend, not the foe, of religion, and Christianity has always enrolled among her adherents some of the greatest minds of the world. At the same time, dull intellects do not penetrate any subject, and of course do not encounter those obstacles in the search after truth which sometimes throw others into a state of hesitancy and unrest.

One day, as Harry was in the field helping "Priest Wood" do his haying, the case of Pharaoh presented itself, and God's decrees and dealings with him, and Harry said to himself, "If the Lord raised him up for this purpose, and hardened his heart, how was he to blame?" At dinner he asked the minister to explain this. The old "priest" shook his head, and said, "Harry, you have got hold of a tough subject, and had better let it alone."

This did not satisfy Harry, and he pressed the conversation until he got some light upon the heart-hardening spoken of. The good man stated that God simply did *not soften* Pharaoh's heart, and added, "God is said to harden the heart when he withholds restraining grace—to harden when he does not soften. He is said to make blind when he does not enlighten, as freezing and darkness follow upon the absence of the sun, the source of light and heat." He farther said, "If you should take a sapling, and twist and bend it, but not quite *break* it, it would be the tougher for the wrenching it had had, and you might fairly be said to have *hardened* the sapling. So was this wicked king's heart hardened by God's providences, which bent but did not break him."

The minister farther told Harry that the question he had raised involved the matter of God's sovereignty and its harmony with man's free agency, and that this was too deep a question for us to understand. He quoted a verse from the Bible which helped Harry a good deal, namely: "The secret things belong unto the Lord our God; but things which are revealed belong unto us."

An item of advice from Martin Luther to his friend and coadjutor, Philip Melanchthon, which Harry met with about that time, was also of advantage to him. It was this: "Philip, do be content to let God know some things you don't know."

But it was impossible for one constituted like

Harry not to keep on thinking, and Satan took advantage of the coldness of his heart to ply him with awful doubts, until he was mentally one of the most miserable of mortals. He even went so far as to half question the very existence of a God. It was only for a moment, however, that he was able to do it. The hardest difficulty he met in getting rid of the idea of a God was his own consciousness. He *felt* God within his breast. In sober moments he was afraid of God, and trembled before him. And in this Harry only experienced what every human being, even a heathen, experiences; for the sentiment of God, the apprehension of him, the belief of a supreme power, is universal. And this is one of the proofs of his existence.

Another stubborn difficulty which Harry met in the atheistic theory was the creation and direction of the material world. The apostle Paul says, in the first chapter of Romans, that the heathens are without excuse for not knowing and obeying God, for the things that they see all around them "declare his eternal power and Godhead." To Harry's mind it seemed that this must be so, and he would stand of a glorious night, and looking up into the clear blue sky, studded with its countless gems, repeat Addison's lines:

> "What though in solemn silence all
> Move round this dark terrestrial ball?
> What though nor real voice nor sound
> Amid their radiant orbs be found?
>
> "In Reason's ear they all rejoice,
> And utter forth a glorious voice,
> For ever singing, as they shine,
> 'The hand that made us is divine.'"

It also seemed to him that the opening and closing parts of Mrs. Sigourney's "No God" were very beautiful:

> "'No God! No God!' the simplest flower
> That on the wild is found
> Shrinks as it drinks its cup of dew,
> And trembles at the sound:
> 'No God!' astonished Echo cries
> From out her cavern hoar,
> And every wandering bird that flies
> Reproves the atheist lore.
>
> "'No God!' with indignation high
> The fervent sun is stirred,
> And the pale moon turns paler still
> At such an impious word!
> And, from their burning thrones, the stars
> Look down with angry eye,
> That thus a worm of dust should mock
> ETERNAL MAJESTY!"

A man in the neighborhood, who pretended to be an atheist, told Harry that the matter of which the world is made is eternal.

"That is absurd," replied Harry, "for if eternal it must be self-existent, and the attribute of self-existence would imply nothing less than the idea of a God. Besides," he added, "who sustains the world?"

"Attraction," answered the skeptic.

"But will you tell me what attraction is?" demanded Harry. The man was silent. "And how came the particles of that tree, and that leaf, and this body of mine, to arrange themselves into such curious and various forms?"

"Chance did it," replied the man.

"But tell what you *mean* by chance," Harry quickly answered. And again the man was silent.

Harry added, "I have ten books at home in my little library, and to print them correctly millions of letters must be used. Each of these millions must be exactly in its own place or there will be a mistake. Now, suppose you should pick up these books in a field, far away from any house. Who could believe that *chance* set the type, and printed, and bound, and laid these books there? Yet all this might be done by chance more easily than the world and all things in it could be made by chance!"

We see by this that it was impossible for Harry to embrace the doctrine of atheism. Nor was it strange. Some years ago a Frenchman who, like many of his countrymen, had won a high rank among men of science, yet who denied the God who is the Author of all science, was crossing the great Sahara in company with an Arab guide. He noticed, with a sneer, that at certain times his guide, whatever obstacles might arise, put them all aside, and kneeling on the burning sand, called on his deity.

Day after day passed and still the Arab never failed, till at last one evening the philosopher, when he rose from his knees, asked him, with a contemptuous smile,

"How do you know there is a God?"

The guide fixed his burning eye on the scoffer for a moment in wonder, and then said, solemnly,

"How do I know that there is a God? How did I know that a camel and not a man passed by my hut last night in the darkness? Was it not by the *print of his foot* in the sand? Even

Harry's Conflicts.

Page 41.

so"—and he pointed to the sun, whose last rays were flashing over the lonely desert—"that footprint is *not* that of a man!"

An intelligent young pagan who had been taught that the world was self-produced came to confront one of our missionaries. The missionary took out a little tin box, called the betel-box.

"What is that?" the young man asked.

"A tin box," was the reply.

"That is all, is it?"

"Yes."

"And it is of very trifling value?"

"Yes."

"Now, could that little box fashion itself into its present shape?"

"No, of course not; some man made it so."

"You are satisfied of that, are you?"

"Yes, fully."

"Now, if that little worthless box could not fashion itself into its present form, how can you suppose that this world, with the sun and moon and stars, and all that we see, brought itself into being?"

That simple thought pierced him like an arrow, and from that moment he was miserable until he found the true God and his Son Jesus Christ.

It may be doubted whether the world has ever seen a real atheist. A man once affirmed, and over and over again, that he was one. A minister asked him if he would stand any test he would put him to in proof of sincerity.

"Yes," he answered; "what do you propose?"

"This night," said the minister, "when deep sleep shall fall upon man, and thick darkness shall cover the world, you shall, taking solemn thought, and after deep meditation, walk deliberately and alone to yonder hill, and in the thick darkness of the forest which covers its summit you shall stand and raise your eyes and clenched hands to the firmament above you, and shall then declare, 'There is no God who created me; there is no God who preserves me; there is no God whom I fear.' Will you do this?"

The atheist was confounded with the proposition.

"Oh," said the minister, "you are no atheist. I was sure you were mistaken. We agree on this point. There is no place for argument."

Coleridge has well depicted the determination

of some not to believe, and their self-imposed blindness:

> "The owlet Atheism,
> Forth from his dark and lonely hiding-place
> Sailing on obscure wings athwart the noon,
> Drops his blue-fringed lids and holds them close,
> And hooting at the glorious sun in heaven,
> Cries out, '*Where is it?*'"

Harry was also greatly troubled in mind about the doctrine of the Trinity, and he asked " Priest Wood" to explain how three persons could dwell in one, and one in three, being at the same time three and one. The answer he received was about this:

"I am not bound to explain everything concerning God, and, indeed, we cannot explain many things about ourselves; but I can prove there is a Trinity in Deity by that infallible standard of all truth, the Holy Bible."

"How?" asked Harry.

"In this way," answered the parson. "Three persons in the Godhead are invoked in the apostolic benediction. The titles God, Jehovah, etc. are given equally to three persons in the Godhead. They are represented as possessing equal knowledge, power, etc. Divine works are also ascribed to the three persons. The same is true of divine worship." He farther said, "'Canst thou by searching find out God? Canst thou find out the Almighty to perfection?' Since the fact of the divine Trinity is revealed, we should believe it, even though it is, in some respects, beyond our comprehension."

But about this time there moved into town a family from Boston who held the belief of the Unitarians, that the Saviour, while more than human, is less than divine. The head of the family was a very upright man, and more intelligent than most people, and it gave Harry great satisfaction to converse with him upon topics of religion. Compelled to admit the force of Mr. Wood's reasoning as to the Trinity, it yet remained a mystery which, as it seemed to him, the denial of Christ's divinity would help to solve.

This view of the case was stated to the good "orthodox" preacher one day by Harry, with the remark that he saw nothing objectionable in the belief of the Unitarians.

"Are you still at your habit of querying?" demanded the parson. "Why can you not let knotty questions alone?" He also quoted a saying of one of the Greek philosophers, "Were

I fully able to describe God, I should be God myself, or God must cease to be what he is." And also the converted Indian's explanation of Deity in humanity: "When Jesus came into the world, he threw his blanket around him, but the God was within still."

The preacher farther remarked, "I have read history, as far back as there is any written history, and I find that from the first our Saviour was honored, and worshiped too, by his followers, as very God. So common was it among the early Christians to pay religious homage to Christ that it was usual to distinguish them by this circumstance. Pliny, governor of Bithynia, in a letter to the emperor Trajan, says he had made inquiries concerning the Christians, and learned 'that they were accustomed, on a stated day, to meet before daylight, and to sing with one another a hymn to Christ as God.' Eusebius, proving the opinion that Christ is a mere man to be a departure from the primitive faith, quotes a writer still more ancient as saying, 'Moreover, all the psalms and hymns of the brethren, written from the beginning by the faithful, celebrate the praises of Christ, the Word of God, and attribute divinity to him.' Now," added the parson, "all these were idolaters, unless Christ be God."

Just as Harry was turning to go away, the excellent man said, "Harry, hold a moment; I want to tell you that *three books* testify to the actual divinity of Christ."

"*What* three books?" said Harry.

"The book of *your own heart*," he replied, "for believers *feel* and *know* that Christ is none other than God; and the book of God's *universe*. The *heavens* gave witness, a new star passing through the sky at his incarnation, and at his crucifixion for three hours the sun was extinguished. The *winds* and *seas* gave witness, when at his word the furious tempest was hushed and the billows smoothed into a dead calm; at the same word the inhabitants of the waters crowded round the ship, and filled the net of the astonished and worshiping disciples. The *earth* gave witness: at his death and at his resurrection it trembled to its centre. *Diseases* gave witness: fevers were rebuked; issues of blood were stanched; the blind saw their Deliverer; the deaf heard his voice; the dumb published his glory; the sick of the palsy were made whole; and the lepers were cleansed at his bidding. And he performed these wonders in his *own name*, and by *his own authority*, while all others who wrought miracles did it in the name of another, even of God. The *grave* gave witness when Lazarus came forth, and when many bodies of the saints which slept arose. The *invisible world* gave witness. Devils acknowledged his divinity, and flew to the abodes of misery, and angels ministered unto him in the desert, the garden, and the tomb, and worshiped him at his advent."

"What is the other book that testifies to Christ's divinity?" asked Harry.

"The *Bible;* and I have here drawn off some of the names, titles given to Christ in the Scriptures, which I advise you to keep, and carefully examine." Upon this he handed him a slip of paper, which was of great service in settling Harry's mind upon the true attitude of Christ in revelation. Upon it was printed, substantially, the following: "Christ, *spoken of* as Jehovah (*Lord*), as Jehovah of glory, as Jehovah our righteousness, as Jehovah above all, as Jehovah the First and the Last, as Jehovah's fellow and equal, as Jehovah of hosts, as Jehovah of David the shepherd, as Jehovah for whose glory all things were created, as Jehovah the Messenger of the covenant; *invoked as* Jehovah, as the eternal God and Creator, as the mighty God, as the great God and Saviour, as God over all, as the true God, as God the Word, as God the Judge, as Emmanuel, as King of kings and Lord of lords, as the Holy One, as the Lord from heaven, as the Lord of the Sabbath, as Lord of all, as Son of God, as the only begotten Son of the Father; his blood is called the blood of God, as one with the Father, as sending the Spirit equally with the Father, as entitled to equal honor with the Father, as Owner of all things equally with the Father, as unrestricted by the law of the Sabbath equally with the Father, as unsearchable equally with the Father, as Creator of all things, as Supporter and Preserver of all things, as possessed of the fullness of the Godhead, as raising the dead, as raising himself from the dead; as eternal, as omnipresent, as omnipotent, as omniscient, as discerning the thoughts of the heart, as unchangeable, as having power to forgive sins, as giving pastors to the church; as Husband of the church, as the object of divine worship, as the object of Faith.

As God, too, he redeems and purifies the church unto himself; and as God he presents the church unto himself, while saints live unto him as God."

In a subsequent conversation, Harry's attention was called to the fact that unless Christ were divine he could not, by his obedience and death, have taken away the sin of the world; for if a created being, then all he could have done would have been simply a matter of due; he had owed it all to God, and therefore could not have brought in merit for offenders. So that if we do away with Christ's divinity, we must do away also with the doctrine of atonement, and are at once upon the most dangerous ground.

By this time Harry felt himself compelled to accept the orthodox faith in regard to the Redeemer of man, if the Scriptures be considered our guide. And a couple of incidents which he met with in a religious paper seemed very forcible as bearing in this direction. One was a conversation of Daniel Webster with several distinguished gentlemen, in which Mr. Webster was asked if he could comprehend how Jesus Christ could be both God and man. "No, sir," he replied, and added, "I should be ashamed to acknowledge him as my Saviour if I could comprehend him. If I could comprehend him, he would be no greater than myself. Such is my sense of sin and consciousness of my inability to save myself, that I feel I need a superhuman Saviour, one so great and glorious that I cannot comprehend him."

The other circumstance was this: Two gentlemen were disputing on the divinity of Christ. One of them, who argued against it, said,

"If it were true, it certainly would have been expressed in unequivocal terms."

"Well," said the other, "admitting that you believed it, and were to teach it, how would you express the doctrine?"

"I would say that Jesus Christ is the true God."

"You are very happy," replied the other, "in the choice of your words, for John, speaking of the Son, says, 'This is the true God, and eternal life.'"

He was also much impressed with this remarkable passage which he met with in a life of Napoleon Bonaparte. In a conversation with Count de Montholon, at St. Helena, he said,

"I know men, and I tell you that Jesus is not a man. The religion of Christ is a mystery which subsists by its own force, and proceeds from a mind which is not a human mind. We find in it a marked individuality, which originated a train of words and actions unknown before. Jesus is not a philosopher, for his proofs are miracles, and from the first his disciples adored him. Alexander, Cæsar, Charlemagne, and myself founded empires, but on what foundation did we rest the creations of our genius? Upon force. Jesus Christ founded an empire upon love, and at this hour millions of men would die for him. I die before my time, and my body will be given back to the earth to become food for worms. Such is the fate of him who has been called the great Napoleon. What an abyss between my end and the eternal kingdom of Christ, which is proclaimed, loved, and adored, and is extending over the whole earth!" Turning to General Bertrand, the emperor added, "If you do not perceive that Jesus Christ is God, I did wrong to appoint you general."

Later in life, Harry used often to repeat this verse of an old hymn, as very just and impressive:

> "What think ye of Christ? is the test
>   To try both your state and your scheme:
> You cannot be right in the rest
>   Unless you think rightly of him."

But these mental agitations on the part of Harry were mere skirmishes compared with a fiercer battle that was raging within between truth and error, involving even the question whether the supreme Ruler of the world has ever revealed himself to men. Shut up to the conviction that there is a God, he yet asked, "Is the Bible really a communication from God to the inhabitants of this world?" "How do I know it?" "How can it be proved?" And the difficulty was much increased by his falling upon two or three infidel works just then, which he kept out of sight, but carefully read.

His father, who was a minister, was exceedingly surprised and grieved at the indications of this tendency of Harry's mind, and determined to use every effort to counteract it. Interrogated as to whether this was the case, Harry frankly admitted the fact, but added that he was sincere, and only wanted to get at the truth.

"Have you ever examined the proofs that the Bible is the word of God?" asked the father.

"No, sir," said Harry. "If there are any, I do not know what they are; and it would please me exceedingly to ascertain them."

"Then come into the study some time, and we

will see whether there are any proofs," said the father.

The next evening found Harry and his father sitting in the study, and Harry proposed to take up the subject in good earnest.

"Not quite yet," said the good minister; "let us first seek the help of God;" and so saying, he knelt and sought the divine guidance. "Now take that book," said the father, handing him a copy of the New Testament, "and I will prove to you that that volume is from God. We will take one step at a time, and the first thing to be settled is, whether the books in the New Testament were really written by the men and at the time generally supposed."

From this point the conversation went on much as follows:

Father. Is there any doubt that such a personage as Jesus Christ did once live on the earth?

Son. I suppose there is not; even the boldest of infidels have never denied it.

F. Is there any doubt as to the time when, and the place where, he lived?

S. Not so far as I know; this is never called in question.

F. Is there not as good ground for believing

that he lived when and where it is affirmed that he did as for believing that Cicero, or Cæsar, or Alexander, lived when and where *they* did?

S. We will admit it.

F. Saying nothing now of the testimony of the Scriptures, could any historical fact be more fully established?

S. I suppose not.

F. Is it not equally certain that Matthew and Mark, and Peter and Paul, etc., lived when and where it is generally supposed they lived?

S. It is, so far as I am aware. But supposing that these men lived, and at the time generally supposed—that is, about eighteen hundred years ago—what evidence is there that the books of the New Testament were written then and by them?

F. There is abundant testimony that they were written then and by these men, in the writings of those who lived in the days of the apostles and were their companions; and it is also confirmed in the writings of those who immediately succeeded them, since they are often quoted by the Christian Fathers of the first centuries as the genuine works of those whose names they now bear.

S. Do you mean to say that there is an unbroken succession of testimony to this effect, by Christian writers, from the times of the apostles until now?

F. I do; and there is evidence on this point in the writings of the early enemies of Christianity themselves. The Scriptures are often referred to by them, and they universally admitted that they were the genuine productions of those to whom they are now ascribed.

S. I have heard that there were very early translations of these books into different languages—as early as the first or second century. Were they, in these translations, ascribed to the same origin as now?

F. They were, precisely.

S. Is there evidence in the books of the New Testament themselves that they are genuine?

F. There is. For instance, the incidental descriptions of the age and country which they contain are such as could have been given by none but writers who lived at that time, and there is a remarkable incidental agreement between these writings and the ascertained events and circumstances of the times. Let me ask you, then, what two facts concerning the books of the New Testament are thus far clearly established?

S. The fact that they were written by the men to whom, and at the time to which, they are ascribed.

F. Is there a single work, in all the writings of the ancient Greeks and Romans, the age and origin of which are established by such conclusive evidence as that of the New Testament?

S. So far as I know of there is not.

F. You are entirely correct in this belief.

S. But what evidence is there that the writers of the New Testament gave a *true account* of the history, character, and doctrines of Christ?

F. Their means of information were ample, and they could have had no possible motive for deception.

S. Did the early Christians receive all the writings of the New Testament as true?

F. They did.

S. Were they acknowledged as authentic by the *enemies* of Christianity?

F. They were—they never denied this; and this is a sufficient proof that they were not a fictitious or false narrative. Suppose a book were now to make its appearance purporting to contain a record of events that occurred one or two hundred years since, and as remarkable as those narrated in the New Testament, but that the whole was a mere fabrication. You see that it would not be possible that it should be universally received as an authentic history, even by the people among whom it stated that the events occurred.

S. Do you, then, affirm that no history of remote ages comes to us so well authenticated as the New Testament?

F. I do; and is it not exceedingly unreasonable to admit the veracity of other early histories, some of which were written before Christ, and yet deny the authenticity of the New Testament? Besides, there is the evidence in the books of the New Testament themselves that they are true—for instance, a perfect harmony exists in the statements of the different writers, though they evidently wrote independently of each other, and there is an appearance of sincerity and fidelity in the style and manner of the writers. These things compelled even the infidel Rousseau to say that "the history of Socratès, which nobody presumes to doubt, is not so well attested as that of Jesus Christ."

S. But how about the Old Testament?

F. There is no doubt that certain writings which we call the Old Testament Scriptures were in existence at the time of Christ. This is universally admitted. And the translation of the Old Testament into Greek, commonly called the Septuagint, or translation of the Seventy, was made three hundred years previous to the birth of Christ.

S. What evidence is there that the books of the Old Testament which *we have* are the identical books *then* extant?

F. This is proven by the numerous quotations from them in the New Testament; by the writings of Josephus, the Jewish historian; and by various catalogues of the books of the Old Testament left by early writers, some of which date back as early as the second and third centuries. Moreover, in the numerous references which Christ and his apostles made to the Old Testament, they always referred to it as of divine authority, and it was not possible for them to mistake its age and origin. All this establishes, beyond question, the genuineness and authenticity of the Old Testament Scriptures.

S. Did the entire Jewish nation receive them

as genuine and of divine origin, and do all Jews *now* receive them as such?

F. The Jews have always received them as such. And is it supposable that the entire Jewish people should have been deceived as to the writers of these books and the time when they were written? Besides this, the most distinguished writers of pagan antiquity acknowledged their genuineness and authenticity, while the books themselves afford ample evidence on this point.

S. But how shall we know that these books of the Bible were *inspired*, or *God-given?*

F. The nature of the truths which they communicated was such that they must have been taught them of God; the writers of the Scriptures claimed to be inspired, and Paul says that "all Scripture is given by inspiration of God." Remember, too, that we have already proved that the writers of the Scriptures were honest men and spoke the truth; they could not, therefore, have intentionally asserted what was not true, nor could they have been deceived in respect to their having been inspired; so that we must take their testimony as positive proof of their inspiration.

S. I have thought that no books are so sublime as parts of the Bible; is there any proof in this?

F. There is, for we cannot account for the sublimity of their style and the purity of their doctrines on any other grounds. And what is even more, the writers of the Bible lived in different centuries and different places, yet there is a perfect agreement between them all in what they have written.

S. How about miracles?

F. They are a proof of the divine authority of one's mission and teachings. The fact that the prophets and apostles wrought miracles is equivalent to God's own testimony that their doctrines were of divine origin. Then the writers of the Scriptures often predicted future events, many of which have already come to pass. I ought also to add that the blessed effects of the Bible upon individual and national character prove it to be from heaven; besides, we have the believer's own consciousness, or internal conviction, of its heavenly origin.

S. It seems to me that these points are well taken; but have we conclusive evidence that the books of the Bible have been preserved free from material errors or alterations since they left the hands of their respective authors?

F. We have. The Jews were extremely sedulous in their efforts to preserve the manuscripts of the Old Testament in their original integrity, and they exercised the utmost care in transcribing them, comparing the transcriptions with the original, and even numbering the words and the letters. Josephus asserts that there was such a veneration of the Jews for the sacred Scriptures that no one, down to his time, dared to add or take away anything from them, or even to make the least alteration. Besides, you know that Christ, and the later prophets before him, brought many serious charges against the Jews, but they never charged them with mutilating the Scriptures, nor even intimated it.

S. But may not alterations have been later made?

F. Is it supposable that good men, since the time of Christ, would have altered the Old Testament? And Christians have never charged the Jews with doing it; nor is it possible that it should have been done by any individual or company of individuals without detection by either Christians or Jews, especially since copies have been so numerous and so widely scattered.

S. What evidence is there that we have the *New Testament* as it was first written, or free from corruption?

F. The multiplication of copies in the original language, and of versions or translations, and their frequent private and public reading, rendered it impossible that any material and general alteration should have been made; and Christians from the first have entertained a reverence for the Scriptures, and a sense of the guilt of adding to or taking from them. Moreover, from an early period there have been sects, or parties, among professed Christians, and an attempt on the part of one to mutilate the word of God would have been surely noticed and made known by those who differed from them. Besides this, there is a remarkable agreement between them and all the quotations made from them by early writers, and also a general agreement of all the manuscripts and versions of the New Testament now extant; so close is this agreement that the worst manuscript extant does not misrepresent one article of faith or destroy one moral precept.

The effect of this conversation upon the mind of Harry was wonderful. He had been led through an entirely new field of thought, and the objections to a revelation which he had fancied to be substantial were swept away like spiders' webs by the foot of the traveler. He remarked to his father at close of that evening's talk,

"I am perfectly satisfied; the chain of evidence in confirmation of the claims of the Bible is complete; and I count this, next to that of my conversion, the greatest evening of my life."

He fully appreciated a sentence from Dryden, which he soon, for the first time, met with:

> "Whence but from heaven could men unskilled in arts,
> In several ages born, in several parts,
> Weave such agreeing truths? or how, or why,
> Should all conspire to cheat us with a lie?—
> Unasked their pains, ungrateful their advice,
> Starving their gain, and martyrdom their price."

Indeed, it seemed to Harry after this that the difficulties attending the infidel scheme were a hundred fold greater than those attending the Christian scheme; and this is a true view. Speaking of the Old Testament, the infidel Rousseau said, "The inventor would be a more astonishing character than the hero."

A noted infidel was once advised by his friend to read the Bible to see if it was not true.

"And where shall I begin?" inquired the unbeliever; "at the New Testament?"

"No," said the other; "at the beginning—at Genesis."

The infidel bought a commentary, went home, and sat down to the serious study of the Scriptures. He applied all his strong and well-disciplined powers of mind to try rigidly, but impartially, its truth. As he went on in the perusal he received occasional calls from his professional friend. The infidel freely remarked upon what he had read, and stated his objections. He liked this passage, he thought that touching and beautiful, but he could not credit a third.

One evening the Christian lawyer called and found the unbeliever at home walking the room with a dejected look, his mind apparently absorbed in thought. He continued busily to trace and retrace his steps, not noticing that any one had come in. His friend at length spoke.

"You seem, sir," said he, "to be in a brown study. Of what are you thinking?"

"I have been reading," replied the infidel, "the Moral Law."

"Well, what do you think of it?"

"I will tell you what I used to think," answered the infidel. "I supposed that Moses was the leader of a horde of banditti; that, having a strong mind, he acquired great influence over a superstitious people, and that on Mount Sinai he played off some sort of fireworks, to the amazement of his ignorant followers, who imagined, in their mingled fear and superstition, that the exhibition was supernatural."

"But what do you think now?" interposed his friend.

"I have been looking," said the infidel, "into the nature of that law. I have been trying to see whether I can add anything to it, or take anything from it, so as to make it better. Sir, I cannot. It is perfect. And I have been thinking," he proceeded, "where did Moses get that law? I have read history. The Egyptians and the adjacent nations were idolaters, so were the Greeks and Romans; and the wisest and best Greeks or Romans never gave a code of morals like this. Where did Moses get this law which surpasses the wisdom and philosophy of the most enlightened ages? He lived at a period comparatively barbarous, but he has given a law in which the learning and sagacity of all subsequent time can detect no flaw. Where did he get it? He could not have soared so far above his age as to have devised it himself. I am satisfied where he obtained it. It must have come from heaven. I am convinced of the truth of the religion of the Bible." This was the only reasonable view.

Charles the Second, hearing Vossius, a celebrated infidel, repeating some incredible story, said, "He believes everything but the Bible." This would seem to be true of all infidels. They are really far more credulous than those they scoff at for believing the Scriptures. Some one has admirably put this case as follows:

"You profess to be a freethinker. Now think freely enough for once to observe the following marvelous peculiarities of your scheme:

"You cannot believe the Bible, yet you can believe that a book of the purest morality was contrived by impostors.

"You believe that the noblest and loveliest of all virtuous characters, Jesus Christ, was imagined and drawn by designing men or weak enthusiasts, in a dark and degraded and only half-civilized nation.

"You believe that, in the very age when these things are alleged to have happened, thousands who were competent to know the facts were either misled themselves or combined to mislead others.

"You believe that these fabricators, in vast numbers, submitted to cruel deaths in attestation of these falsehoods.

"You believe that, without patronage of government or power of the sword, this delusion spread itself over a large part of the earth.

"You believe that the lands where this delusion prevailed have been the most civilized, the most virtuous, and the most philanthropic which the world has seen.

"You believe that this scheme of imposture, or delusion, succeeded in supplanting the heathen superstitions of ages wherever it came.

"You believe that thousands of persons are now living who find in this system their chief consolation under trouble, and their chief security against the fear of death.

"You believe that the doctrines which you

reject have been examined and adopted by a large proportion of the most sober, and philosophic, and learned, and sincere minds that have ever existed.

"You believe that there is not on earth any system of truth which has greater claims to the character of a divine revelation than Christianity; and, consequently, that man is *without* any revelation.

"You believe that when you come to die you will have no certainty or assurance with regard to anything beyond the grave.

"You believe, therefore, a mass of difficulties more incapable of explanation than all the wonders of revelation."

No one can doubt the soundness of this position.

There was another thing which very much impressed Harry. He found by examining a book loaned to him by his teacher, containing sketches of the lives and deaths of noted infidels, that they did not really believe what they pretended to believe, as was proved by their honest confessions, especially in the hour of death.

"There is one thing," said Mr. S. to a companion in sin and skepticism, "which mars all the pleasures of my life."

"Ah!" replied the other; "what is that?"

"Why, I am afraid the Bible is true. If I could but certainly know that death is an eternal sleep, I should be happy; my joy would be complete. This is the sword that pierces my very soul. If the Bible be true, I am lost for ever; every prospect is gone; surely I am lost ever! Oh, that 'IF!'"

A company of cavilers once called on a dying friend, one of their number, and stated afterward that they had called to see him, and actually *told him* that they came for that purpose, to advise him now to embrace Christianity: "*Because*," said they, "if it be false, it can do you no harm; but if it should prove true, you will be a great gainer."

Colonel Ethan Allen, who had written several books setting forth objections to the Christian religion, evinced his distrust in his own arguments on an occasion that put him fairly to the test. While once reading some of his writings to a friend who was on a visit at his house, he received information that his daughter was at the point of death. His wife was a pious woman, and had anxiously instructed the daughter in the principles of Christianity. When the colonel appeared at the bedside of his child, she appealed to him thus:

"I am about to die, father; shall I believe in the principles you have taught me, or shall I believe in what my mother has taught me?"

At this question he was much agitated. A deep and solemn conflict passed within, but after waiting a few minutes in silence, he replied,

"Believe in what your mother has taught you."

One has thus sketched the affecting scene of this answer:

> "The frown upon the warrior brow
>   Passed like a cloud away,
> And tears coursed down the rugged cheek
>   That flowed not till that day.
> 'Not, not in mine!' with choking voice
>   The skeptic made reply;
> 'But in thy *mother's* holy faith,
>   My daughter, may'st thou die!'"

Volney, a French infidel, was on board a vessel during a violent storm; when the ship was in imminent danger of being lost, he threw himself on the deck, crying in agony, "O my God! my God!"

"There is a God, then?" said one of the passengers.

"Oh yes, there is! Lord, save me."

The ship came safely to port, and Volney was disconcerted when his confession was publicly related, but he excused it by saying he was so frightened that he did not know what he said!

In spite of all the infidel philosophers who flocked around Voltaire in the first days of his illness, he gave signs of wishing to return to that God whom he had so often blasphemed. He called for the priest, and afterward made a written declaration in which he renounced infidelity, signed by himself and two witnesses. He refused to see his infidel friends, and called upon the Lord Jesus. At one time he was discovered trying to pray. He had fallen from his bed in convulsive agonies, and lay foaming with impotent despair on the floor, when he exclaimed,

"Will not this God whom I have denied save me too? Cannot infinite mercy be extended to me?"

His physician, called to administer relief, retired, declaring the death of the impious man to be terrible indeed. The marshal of Richelieu flew from the bedside, declaring that the sight of such a deathbed was appalling. Voltaire offered the doctor half he possessed if he would prolong his life six months. When the doctor told him he would not live six weeks, "Then," said he, "I shall go to hell, and you will go with me." Soon after he expired. A man who attended him, some years after, said, " I was the nurse that attended Voltaire in his last illness, and for all the wealth of Europe I would never see another infidel die."

In all this we see how the heart repudiates infidelity as impious and absurd. Thus the couplet of Dr. Young is true:

> "Our infidels are Satan's hypocrites;
> Pretend the worst, and at the bottom fail."

It is also worthy of remark that the moral effects of the scheme of infidelity are unquestionably bad. Lord Barrington once asked Collins, the infidel writer, how it was that, though he seemed to have very little religion himself, he took so much care that his servants should attend regularly at church. He replied, "To prevent their robbing or murdering me." To such a character, how applicable are these words: "Out of thine own mouth will I judge thee!"

Cook, who was executed for a very awful murder at Leicester, in England, in his confession allowed that his associates were deists, that they frequented a public-house in which the writings of Paine, Carlisle, and other infidel writers were read. He emphatically added: "I considered myself a moral man, attending Christian worship three times a day, until I became an infidel."

When an infidel production was submitted, probably by Paine, to Benjamin Franklin, in manuscript, he returned it to the author with a letter from which the following is extracted: "I would advise you not to attempt *unchaining the tiger*, but to burn this piece before it is seen by any other person. If men are so wicked with religion, what would they be without it?"

The writer cannot too earnestly warn the young against being influenced by any attacks on the sacred Scripture. It rests on a rock. No book has begun to be so opposed as the Bible, and it has been subjected to every possible test, yet it stands. Some time ago, as one has remarked, every man who had a smattering of science discovered among its first axioms that Genesis was a fable and Christianity a dream.

Some peering fool, using a very imperfect telescope, peeped into the sky and saw vestiges of every body in the universe, but none of God. Another dug into the bowels of the earth and brought up beautiful gems and sparkling ores, but upon none of the gems could any one discover the autograph of revelation—on none of the ores the beauty and glory of him who made it. Another proved that mankind had some half dozen, or perhaps twelve dozen, original parents, and that the notion of our being descended from Adam and Eve was a joke, a mere myth, the vagary of a doting person called Moses.

But what are seen to be the facts now? Astronomy, geology, ethnology, all science, and all discovery come forward to attest to the claims of revelation. Even the old mummies, the dumb pyramids, and the mounds and the ashes of ruined cities are eloquent in its behalf. At a recent meeting held in London for the purpose of establishing a museum for the illustration of the Holy Scriptures, Sir Henry Rawlinson, distinguished for his researches at Nineveh, said that he had been enabled to trace Oriental records, by means of the monumental inscriptions now in the British Museum, from the time of Abraham's departure from Ur of the Chaldees down to that of Alexander the Great, a period of two thousand years; and that whenever the course of the history came alongside that of the Jewish people, there was an absolute coincidence between these records and the details of Scripture—the same names, the same successions of kings, the same facts.

The Bible lasts, then. You need not be concerned about that. Every argument against it has been exploded a thousand times. Paine, in his low and ribald language, once said,

"I have gone up and down through the Christian garden of Eden, and with my simple axe I have cut down one after another of its trees till I have scarcely left a single sapling standing."

What would he think were he alive now, when Christianity is belting, with its girdle of light, the globe?

The tomb of the celebrated infidel, David Hume, is a circular stone building in Edinburgh, and over its iron-grated door is inscribed his name, with the date of his birth and death. The other tablets in the tomb show that, though he thought he had given the death-blow to Christianity, he was unable to induce his relatives to deny the religion of the gospel; for immediately above his name is an inscription by a David Hume to his wife, dated 1817, closing with these words: "Behold, I come quickly. Thanks be to God, who giveth us the victory through our Lord Jesus Christ." In the interior is another tablet to the memory of another namesake, one of the barons of Exchequer, and his two sons, dated 1848, surmounted by the inspiring words, "I am the resurrection and the life." Thus does God cause even his enemies to praise him.

You need not be ashamed to stand up for the Bible. It honors you more than you can honor it. You can put forward as an argument your *consciousness* of its truth, if nothing more.

> "A man of subtle reasoning asked
> A peasant if he knew
> Where was the internal evidence
> That proved the Bible true.
>
> "The terms of disputative art
> Had never reached his ear;
> He laid his hand upon his heart
> And only answered, 'Here.'"

Let not such evidence be despised.

The following is what a great mind dictated to be inscribed on his tombstone:

"Lord, I believe; help thou mine unbelief. Philosophical argument, especially that drawn from the vastness of the universe in comparison with the apparent insignificance of this globe, has sometimes shaken my reason for the faith which is in me, but my heart has always assured and reassured me that the gospel of Jesus Christ must be a divine reality. The Sermon on the Mount cannot be a merely human production. This belief enters into the very depth of my conscience. The whole history of man proves it.

"Daniel Webster."

An infidel on his deathbed felt himself adrift in the terrible surges of doubt and uncertainty. Some of his friends urged him to hold on to the end, instead of abjuring his faith. "I have no objection to holding on," was the poor man's answer; "but will you tell me what I am to hold on by?" That is the fatal want. If one has thrown away his Bible, what has he to hold on by in the mouth of the yawning abyss? Imagine yourself dying, and ask, "Which has most weight with me now, my cavil or my Bible?"

For another thing, never read skeptical books. A minister called on a young man near the point of death, and in great mental agitation, and told him of Jesus. With an agonizing look, he said, "Ah, sir, but I have rejected the gospel. Some years since, I unhappily read Paine's Age of Reason. It suited my corrupt taste. I embraced its principles. After this, wherever I went, I did all in my power to hold up the Scriptures to contempt. By this means I led others into the fatal snare and made converts to infidelity. Thus I rejected God, and now he rejects me, and will have no mercy on me." The minister offered to pray for him, but he replied, "Oh! now it is all in vain to pray for me." Then, with a dismal groan, he cried out, "Paine's Age of Reason has ruined my soul!" and instantly expired.

Be as careful of introducing moral poison into your mind as you would be of receiving material poison into your body. Eschew it with a stronger abhorrence.

There was one other error to which Harry was exposed. In the town a society of Universalists was formed, and they were very industrious in propagating their doctrines. Much was made of the love of God as a reason why he could not punish eternally the wicked. Harry tried to believe this, and would gladly have done so but for some weak spots which he thought he detected in the theory upon which it rested.

Harry said, "If God is all love and so dislikes suffering that he cannot endure it in his universe, why did he permit sin and suffering to enter the universe? But there is suffering, and so suffering is consistent with the government of a benevolent Being. And if it be consistent with infinite goodness to permit suffering for a few thousand years, while the world stands, why not always?" He thought that the argument drawn from the love of God was, therefore, a fallacy, and did not see why the very love of God itself would not ensure the punishment of the wicked, since he who loves the good must of necessity hate the evil, and be bound to oppose and persecute it.

Harry was also told that men get punished in this world, as they go along. "Then the wickeder men are, the more miserable they are, of course," said he, quickly, in reply; "but I know men so hardened in sin that they don't feel any mental pangs, and they have excellent health, too. Now suppose one of them to be shot through the heart and killed in an instant; what suffering has he had for his life of awful crime and wickedness? That reasoning won't do," said Harry. "The guilty often escape both remorse of conscience and the penalty of human laws. Their eyes stand out with fatness; they have more than heart can wish; they set their mouth against the heavens; they speak wickedly concerning oppression; they speak loftily, and there are no bands in their death. At the same time we see some good people suffering almost everything. How, then, is there a just God, if he do not equalize these matters in another state? Besides this, the Scriptures everywhere teach the doctrine of an eternal retribution."

About this time that eccentric but powerful preacher, John Leland, in one of his missionary tours through New England, came into the town where Harry resided, and made a deep impression by a sermon against Universalism, and some verses which he repeated to show the absurdity of a belief which brought at once into heaven those unfit to live on earth. Here is a part of the production:

> "King Pharaoh and his mighty host
>   Had godlike honors given;
> A pleasant breeze brought them with ease
>   By water into heaven.
>
> "But still the chosen of the Lord
>   Through drought and danger drags;
> They live in fears full forty years,
>   Curst with a thousand plagues.
>
> "Oh yes, God saw them all in sin,
>   And sent that dreadful storm
> To bring them straight to heaven's height,
>   Their manners to reform!
>
> "So all the filthy Sodomites,
>   When God bade Lot retire,
> Went in a trice to Paradise
>   On rapid wings of fire.
>
> "And when the wicked Canaanites
>   To Joshua's host were given,
> The sun stood still so they might kill,
>   And send them on to heaven.
>
> "God saw those nations were too bad
>   To own that fruitful land;
> He, therefore, took the rebels up
>   To dwell at his right hand!

"And Ananias and his wife
    Soon reached the starry throne,
When they in pride had loudly lied
    Unto that sacred One.

"And Judas, that perfidious wretch,
    Was not for crimes accurst;
He by a cord outwent his Lord,
    And got to heaven first!"

The discourse, for a long time, was the town's talk, and did much to counteract a belief which is fast dying out, because it is utterly impossible to reconcile it with common sense and the plain teachings of the Bible.

From these experiences of Harry's with prevailing errors, he became satisfied of two things: one was, that there is no point of assured safety for an inquiring mind between orthodoxy and atheism. Once embrace liberal "sentiments," rejecting the common faith of Christianity, and the way is prepared for accepting any specious error, even to the denial of the existence of the Deity. Cut loose from the obvious teachings of the Bible at any one point, and you may cut loose entirely. Reason was given us to try the evidences of a revelation; when she says these are valid, then *faith* is to be our guide. Not that any revealed truth is *contrary* to reason; but it may be *above* reason. Where we cannot *trace*, there we are to *trust;* even when we cannot fully comprehend what the Bible teaches, we are yet to bow reverentially to its dictates. Christ said, "Blessed are they that have *not seen*, and yet *have believed.*"

The other thing that Harry became satisfied of was this, that skepticism is rather of the heart than the head. We want to believe this or that, and so believe it, as we imagine. The corrupt heart dislikes the truth, and is ready to clutch hold of anything instead: this is the history of liberalism. If Harry's heart had not grown cold toward Christ, he would have been satisfied with "the truth as it is in Jesus;" for—and let this be noted—when, in a short time after these wanderings, upon deep penitence and a reconsecration to the Redeemer, he felt anew his first love, there was no more trouble from doubts. "If any man will do his will, he shall know of the doctrine whether it be of God." "Then shall ye know, if ye follow on to know the Lord." "The secret of the Lord is with them that fear him, and he will show them his covenant."

Duty is the medicine for doubt. Be sure that

your caviling at the doctrines and evidences of Scripture is not a cover for an unwillingness to admit its teachings; in other words, that you do not oppose the Bible because the Bible opposes you, living as you now do. Mr. Wilmot, an infidel, when dying, laid his emaciated hands upon the sacred volume and exclaimed, solemnly and with unwonted energy, "The only objection against this book is—*a bad life.*"

Let that not apply to you. What chance have you if against God and against the Bible? Bow your will to his will, and your understanding to his word. Become a tender-hearted, trustful, loving, and obedient child, and the rest will take care of itself.

> "Ah, how skillful grows the hand
> That obeyeth Love's command!
> It is the heart and not the brain
> That to the highest doth attain;
> And he who followeth Love's behest
> Far excelleth all the rest."

III.

CONTACT WITH THE WORLD.

> "If on our daily course the mind
> Be set to hallow all we find,
> New treasures still, of countless price,
> God will provide for sacrifice;
> The trivial round, the common task,
> Will furnish all we ought to ask—
> Room to deny ourselves, a road
> To bring us nearer unto God."

HARRY found it easy to be a Christian in the prayer-meeting, the closet, and the assembly on the Lord's Day, but quite another thing to keep up the conscious enjoyment of God while in contact with the world. And this is a common experience with Christians. To so combine business and religion as to maintain a spirit of earnest devotion amidst the stir and distraction of every-day duties is one of the most difficult parts of a Christian life.

Some would counsel habitual retirement from the world in order to active devotion. To-day may be seen the caves and other places of concealment in which hermits lived, centuries ago, in the "wilderness" on the banks of the river Jordan, where Christ was tempted forty days. Deluded persons considered it duty thus to retire to solitude, and there are now many who think this the way to be holy.

The Essenes, a sect of the Jews who lived far from the turmoil of their distracted age, on the western shores of the Dead Sea, and who were proud of their caste, their rigid formalism, their quietude, and their self-mortifications, were among the most ancient of those who held this folly. Professedly Christian sects early fell into the same delusion, and from the fourth century, anchorites, or recluses, under the names of monks, nuns, hermits, and the like, appear on the page of history. In the Roman Catholic body, particularly in some of the countries of Europe, the number of these characters is still very great.

There is nothing surprising in this. A contemplative life has its charms. Nothing is so congenial to a particular cast of mind as seclusion, nothing so welcome as some "lodge in the wilderness," some cleft in the rock, some

> "Sacred solitude,
> Where quiet with religion makes her home "—

where the noise and din of wild mortality no more distract the soul which fain would lie calmly in the pavilion of God's presence.

But he who seeks such a life runs athwart the divine order of things. Our Saviour did not pray that his disciples might be taken out of the world. He has nowhere taught us to absent ourselves from human society. Nor has he absolved one of his followers from the obligations to lead an active life. Earth is not a luxurious dormitory. It is designed to be the arena of noble triumph and enduring toil. The gospel does not address men as world-weary recluses. Its precepts and promises come to them as situated amid the annoyances, temptations, and cares of every-day life.

It rebukes some because they "learn to be idle, wandering from house to house." It says to all, Be "not slothful in business;" "study to be quiet, and to do your own business, and work with your own hands;" "if any man will not work, neither let him eat." It represents Christians as the salt of the earth who must diffuse their conservative influence; as the light of the world who are to let their light shine before men; as witnesses for God who must bear testimony in the sight of their fellow-mortals; as stewards who must "occupy" their Lord's goods and "communicate" and "do good unto all men, especially unto them who are of the household of faith."

The very nature and genius of our holy religion discovers the absurdity of the monastic theory. What is Christianity? Not an abstraction, but a power to bless mankind. How, then, can it fulfill its mission unless in its living embodiment it come in contact with men? What is the grand aim of the life of a Christian? To glorify God. And how? By doing good. Shall he then seek the cloister? Shall he abjure human society? Shall he leave the sick to die for want of attention, the ignorant to perish for want of knowledge, and the careless to pass on unwarned into eternity? Is this running into retirement serving God? Far otherwise. That religion which thus divorces business and religion, which spurns contact with the world, and lives only in idle day-dreaming and ecstatic sentimentalism, is not the religion of the Bible.

True religion finds its appropriate sphere

among living, active, thinking men. "It aims," as one has said, "to be at work, working with all, working for all, working everywhere, and working evermore, until the earth be full of the knowledge of the Lord, and the great redeeming work of Calvary shall have won its last soul and garnered its last sheaf."

Devotion, it is true, must have her moments of retirement, but perpetual seclusion is unfriendly to its scope and development. It is as sure to languish in the cloister as is the body amid mephitic vapors.

The history of the monastic orders is proof of this. Rome has fairly tried the experiment, and the results are too patent to be called in question. They are declared in the words of an impartial historian, who says of the monasteries, once so numerous, "It must be admitted that idleness and luxury crept within their walls, together with all the vices of the world, and their decay became inevitable."

No; the religion of Christ is not an exotic that lives only in the soft warmth of the sequestered cell; but rather, though a plant of heavenly origin, it is designed to grow on earthly soil and in the pure sweet air and open sunlight of the skies. Christianity is not a thing to be put on for certain days and occasions, as for the Lord's Day and the sanctuary, and then laid aside, but rather is it to be the accompaniment for all places and all times. Its very essence is love, and it goes out after men that it may do them good. It thrives by beneficence. To shut it up within itself is like attempting to drive the life-blood back into the heart. It is certain death. Its sphere of action is as broad as the world. There is no scene, however homely, where it may not preside, no enterprise, however lofty, which it may not direct. It is to mingle with men as men—mingle in the home, in the market-place, in the workshop, in the counting-house, in the professions, in all the varied phases and conditions of human life.

And it is easy to see why God has ordained that Christians should be thus linked to the world and beset with its cares. One reason is, that craft and fraud may be met and overcome where they exist, and the various evil ingredients of society neutralized by the immediate presence of the good ingredients. Another is, because Christian men are most conspicuous and best appreciated when called out "on the background of secular occupation," just as—to adopt the figure of another—the jewelry of the heavens becomes lustrous because of being set in the night-gloom. But there is a reason beyond all this. It is with a design to the development of a noble type of character; it is that the renewed nature may be strengthened and disciplined and perfected. There are powers that gather force from resistance. Opposing influences are often the most efficient aids to their production and development. "The noblest statue is the visible response which the marble gives back to the blows of the mallet and chisel." So it is with Christian character. The purest models have been formed under the combined influence of God's Spirit and the friction of earthly cares. Temptations have strengthened the power to resist and overcome; patience has been inwrought by sore trials; energy has been matured by antagonism; heavenly-mindedness has been attained by a deeper conviction of the vanity of earthly good; and the rebound of the gracious principle within, consequent upon the pressure of temporal interests without, has given to the whole character a breadth and depth and solidity such as it had never otherwise attained.

A story is told of an elephant upon service in India that, going to drink, fell into the broad deep tank, or well, constructed as a reservoir. To get him out they threw in great quantities of fascines, or bundles, which the intelligent creature placed under his feet as fast as they were given him, and thus raised himself not only to the level of the water, but to the brink of the well, and moved out without difficulty. Now, Satan expects our destruction from being plunged in a sea of anxieties and cares and temptations. But we may make every one of these impediments a means of rising toward heaven and setting ourselves at liberty. Only put them under the feet, and, instead of being overwhelmed by them, they shall help to hoist us out of the well and lift us into paradise. So true is it that our relations to secular pursuits may become productive, not only of nothing harmful, but of much positive good.

We come now to the question, How can fervency of spirit be kept up in a busy life?

As a first condition, make God a party in all your transactions.

Cecil wisely remarks that it is the grand secret of a pious man, in conducting his affairs, that he treats with God about them. This is vastly important to him who would lead a Christian life. But the tendencies are strongly in the opposite direction. Too many "treat with God" only in affairs that are termed religious; in their trades and professions, God is too often practically left out of the question. Some men have a Christian code and a business code—one set of maxims and regulations that looks to religion, and another set that looks to gain; and they plead in justification that it is necessary, in order to success. Others, they say, are not governed by a regard for strict integrity; there is competition in business, and we must not be too nice about moral distinctions. Religion is thus compelled to give way somewhat to the peculiar phases of "the times," and so God is eschewed and forgotten.

Among the heathens the god of traffic was also the god of fraud. The Romans found it convenient to inaugurate theft under the auspices of religion, and one of their poets is thus heard to invoke this goddess:

> "O fair Laverna, grant me power to cheat,
> And yet appear arrayed in saintly guise."

And is not deceit still virtually installed in high

places? Is not the god of this world suffered to give laws for the prosecution of trade? Are not Christian men, perhaps almost unconsciously, influenced by them? There is no positive intention to deceive, but still there is a want of ingenuousness, a want of downright open-handed honesty. There is a keeping back of the truth, or a calling of things by the wrong name. This is labeled as "imported" which never crossed the seas. This is marked "prime" which is known to be third or fourth rate. This is sold for silk which the seller, but not the customer, knows is partly cotton, and this for "the genuine article" which is known to be adulterated, a custom which men smooth over by some soft epithet, but which God rebukes in the words, "Thou shalt not steal."

Now, where God is thus ignored, is it possible to lead a life of piety? This is a direct invitation to the wicked one to come in and subordinate the mind and the affections, and how can it be otherwise than that such individuals should be overcharged with the cares of this world? He who succeeds in this way may expect to be crushed, like Tarpeia of old, by the very weight of his success. Set the Lord always before your face. Consult him as one of the parties in every transaction. If you cannot thus pursue your vocation, then abandon it. Better fail of money-making than fail of pleasing God—than fail of heaven.

It is often remarked that it is impossible for young men to succeed in worldly callings, yet maintain a Christian character. As one represents it, multitudes say, "If I were an old man, and were not perplexed with worldly affairs, I could be a Christian, but the exigencies of business require so many things that are inconsistent with honesty and truth that a secular life is not compatible with Christianity. I am a young man, and am poor, and I must conform to the customs of the community and to public sentiment, or go down. It is a choice between succeeding and failing. If I adhere to rigidity of conscience, I shall have to shut the door, and starve."

But this view is wholly incorrect. If you are called to any place, and you have the natural gifts to sustain yourself in that place, you can sustain yourself better by the most rigid observance of the injunctions of the gospel than by a violation of them. And you that are entering professions, you that are in the midst of pleasures, you that are in the initial steps of business, and are tempted, for the sake of earthly good, to take a lower view of piety,—in that last all-judging day God will show you that you sacrificed your worldly prosperity by the very means by which you attempted to gain it.

It was Henry Clay who said, "I had rather be right than be President."

> "Do what is right, be faithful and fearless,
> Onward, press onward, the goal is in sight;
> Eyes that are wet very soon will be tearless,
> Blessings await you in doing the right.
>
> "Do what is right, let the consequence follow;
> Battle for virtue in spirit and might,
> And with stout hearts look ye forth to the morrow:
> God will protect you in doing the right."

As another help to the maintenance of a vigorous Christian life in the pressure of worldly concerns, bring to your aid the advantages of the appointed means of grace.

There is often a temptation to neglect those means under the plea, "I must attend to my business; and if I make money, I can do a great deal of good with it." So one bends every energy of body and mind to the pursuit of gain.

He is in his counting-room, his store, his office, or his shop early and late. He has no time for meetings, for reading, for social enjoyment, or for doing good to others. He puts all these things off; he hopes to enjoy all and do all by and by, when he gets through the present pressure. He does not mean to work so hard always, or, in plainer terms, he will get rich, and then attend to these other things. But see what is the consequence: he has formed a habit of neglecting the weekly prayer-meetings; he has formed the habit of neglecting the Bible and secret prayer, or attending to those things very slightly; he has found his pleasure in an intense business activity, and will not now find pleasure in anything else. Beware of such a course! Care for your soul first. No Christian has a right to give himself so intensely to business as to interfere with his religion. God first—his claims supreme—and then so much of other things as may be consistent with lively piety and Christian enjoyment and usefulness.

This is the only rule by which the Christian ought to live, whatever may be the allurements to vast business projects or sudden accumulations of wealth. It is nowhere said, "In the sweat of thy brow thou shalt break thy heart, and destroy thy life, and lose thy soul."

Cling, then, to the helps offered in the means of grace. Familiarize yourself with the Bible. Leave it not a day unopened, make it your *vade mecum*, your "go with me," your pocket companion; you need its precepts to enlighten, its counsels to direct, its warnings to restrain, its motives to encourage and persuade. Have your stated seasons of retirement for meditation and prayer. It was a rule of one of the best Christians and most successful merchants in New York, which he adopted in entering upon business, and from which he never deviated, that, whatever his engagements, he would, like the Psalmist, enter three times a day into his closet for private devotion. Let nothing interfere with your seasons of retirement. The very sense of being alone with God will tend to restore the impressions of invisible and spiritual things so necessary to the Christian life, but which continued contact with the world is liable to efface. Retirement will clarify your spiritual atmosphere. Your solitary chamber will furnish a new standpoint from which to look out upon the world, and your relations to it and to eternity.

And what is more, your spiritual impotence will there be clothed upon with God's omnipotence, thus fitting you for life's conflict and for life's trials.

Moreover, avail yourself of the privileges of the Lord's Day. Who can estimate the value of this "pearl of days"? How fragrant its hallowed remembrances! How grateful its rest and sweet repose! How it puts the brake upon life's treadmill, and unclasps the iron hold of the world! How it "repeats the miracle of the Red Sea, and rolls back the swelling tide which threatens to submerge us"! How it opens to us the green pastures and the still waters of the land of promise! Scrupulously observe its sacred hours. On their return bid the world retire and "drive each carnal thought away." Go up to the house of God, and have a place in the house of God—a place which you may esteem your own, and which you will feel called upon to fill.

Again, pursue your worldly affairs with reference to one specific object—the glory of God in the welfare of man. Pursue steadily one great object or aim, whatever your sphere of life. As to a Godward turn of mind, one has rightly said:

> "All may of thee partake:
> Nothing can be so mean
> Which with this purpose,—*for thy sake*,
> Will not grow bright and clean.
>
> "A servant with this clause
> Makes drudgery divine;
> Who sweeps a room as for thy laws
> Makes that and the action fine."

Our Lord taught that where "the eye is single the whole body is full of light." The eye regulates the motion of the members of the body and gives them precision and certainty. Just so the object in view regulates the life. Rope-dancers, in order to steady themselves, fix the eye on some one object and look steadfastly on that. Let the eye or the intention be wrong, and all the energies are misdirected and out of order. If the pilot of a vessel be drowned, and the lights be put out, and the captain be taken prisoner, what hope is there for those on board the ship? In like manner all the powers and faculties of our nature are in disorder or confusion if our aim or intention be wrong. Mark out a circle, and draw the lines from the circumference directly to the centre, and you may draw as many as you please, they will not intersect each other. You cannot run one across the other if all tend to the central point. So let heaven, and this alone, be the object to which one directs his course, and there will be no crossings and inconsistencies in all the lines of his life, however many such lines there may be. But let him live with this world in view as well as the next, and the lines of his character and conduct will surely cross one another.

In theory, the Christian recognizes no personal proprietorship in himself or his possessions. Bought with a price, himself and all belong to God. He reads the imprint and superscription of his Lord upon every fragment of time, and every item of property, and every ounce of influence. Such is his profession, his theory, and such should be his practice. "I have this day been before God," says Edwards, "and have given myself, all that I am and have, to God, so that I am in no respect my own. I can challenge no right in myself, in this understanding, this will, these affections; neither have I a right to this body, or any of its members— no right to this tongue, these hands, these feet, these eyes, these ears: I have given myself clean away." And it was one of Sir Matthew Hale's written rules of life, "To serve God in his ordinary calling, and to mingle somewhat of God in all that he did."

But, practically, is this consecration of business maintained? We read in the old fable, says some writer, of one Midas who turned into gold whatever he touched. But times are changed now, for "touch a man *with* gold, and he will turn to anything." There are exceptions, it is true, which show that money is not omnipotent in the hands of all men. It was a noble saying of a great naturalist who, when urged to deliver a popular lecture, and told that money should not stand in the way, replied, "I cannot afford to waste my time in making money." And there are Christian men who truly do business for God. That model Christian business man, Nathaniel R. Cobb, said, "Not that I would compare money-making, in point of importance, with the preaching of Christ; but I think I can say, as in the sight of God, that my aim in making money is the same as that of every true minister of Christ in preaching the gospel." Shortly after his conversion, he drew up and signed the following paper, wherein lay the secret of his success, and wherein young men beginning business may find a copy fit to follow:

"By the grace of God, I will never be worth over $50,000.

"By the grace of God, I will give one-fourth of the net profits of my business to charitable and religious uses.

"If I am ever worth $20,000, I will give one-half my net profits, and if I am ever worth $30,000, I will give three-fourths, and the whole after $50,000.

"So help me God, or give to a more faithful steward, and set me aside.

"N. R. Cobb."

Here is the way for a pious youth to gain the mastery of money for the service of Christ and humanity; and who may not in this way become an eminent servant of God? The truth is, we draw the lines too sharply between things religious and things secular. In one sense there is no real ground of distinction. When Paul was in Ephesus, was he less really serving God while making tents by lamplight than while disputing in the synagogue, or in the school-room of Tyrannus? May not Abel or David have been really serving the Lord while keeping sheep, or Daniel while acting the statesman, or Luke while attending the sick, or Gaius while entertaining the saints—as truly serving God as when they were engaged in what we call strictly religious duties? Look at Newton "toiling amidst the stars," at Hale before a jury or on the bench of justice; at Jones exploring the Oriental languages; at Wilberforce mingling in the conflicts of policy and debate; at Carey mending the shoes of the English rustics; at Bunyan tagging lace in Bedford jail; at Thornton, or Cobb, or Bleeker, busy among their merchandise; at Page by his carpenter's bench; at Nolmond Smith busy in his manufactory. Who will either deny the eminent attainments of these men in piety or allege that, while occupied in their active pursuits, they may not have been strictly and directly serving the Lord? Men talk of the "sacred professions," but all professions, if they are legitimate and proper, may be, and ought to be, sacred.

Some are called of God to serve in one occupation, some in another, yet each for the great Proprietor's advantage. Some are called to serve at the counter, some at the anvil, some at the loom, some at the carpenter's bench, some at the bench of justice, some by ploughing the deep waters, some by ploughing the warm soil, some by preaching, some by teaching, some with the hand, some with the mouth, some with the brain; but all in every department are bound to make the promotion of religion, either directly or indirectly, their chief business, their great aim. Each should adopt the watchword of the zealous but deluded Loyola: "Ad Majoram Dei Gloriam"—"For the greater glory of God." Men should be "not slothful in business," not to serve themselves, but "serving the Lord." They need not abandon their business that they may serve the Lord, but for that very purpose prosecute it.

It is pleasant to believe that with increasing numbers views like these are being entertained and practiced upon. But what mistakes still prevail in regard to money-making! No one would deny that the accumulation of wealth is to be commended if it be sought with right motives and within proper limits.

Money may be a power for good. It is not necessarily the rich who find it hard to enter the kingdom of heaven, but those that love riches. It is not the money that is the "root of all evil," but the love of money.

The evil, however, lies precisely here, that

wealth is made an end instead of a means to an end. Men seek after a competence, not that they may glorify God, but glorify themselves—not that they may use it for the good of the needy, but squander it for the gratification of pride and the baser passions. They accumulate, not that they may give unto him that asketh, but that they may satiate the cravings of a covetous heart, or perhaps leave a splendid fortune to an idol child, like him of whom one of our own poets hath sung:

> "He hath sold his life to gather gain
> And build a mansion for his only son,
> That crowds might envy. To his wearied heart,
> Amid its slavery, oft he said, "*Plod on;*
> '*Tis for my son,*"

forgetting that that very fortune might prove the curse of the pampered boy, or that, in mercy, God might take him away from the evil to come, leaving one more illustration of the Scripture, "He heapeth up riches, and knoweth not who shall gather them."

It is a beautiful remark of Lord Bacon, "Seek not proud wealth, but such as thou mayest get justly, use soberly, distribute cheerfully, and leave contentedly;" and it was the distinguished

William Wirt who said, "Excessive wealth is neither glory nor happiness. The cold and sordid wretch who thinks only of himself, who draws his head within his shell, and never puts it out but for the purpose of lucre and ostentation,—such a man may be rich, but, trust me, he can never be happy nor virtuous nor great. There is in a fortune a golden mean which is the appropriate region of virtue and intelligence. Be content with that; and if the horn of plenty overflow, let its droppings fall upon your fellow-men, let them fall like the droppings of honey in the wilderness, to cheer the faint and weary pilgrim." If within such limitations, and for worthy purposes, you seek the acquisition of wealth—seek it without setting the heart upon it, without allowing it to prevent the cultivation of the mind and the affections, seek it to possess the means of doing good—then it is every way praiseworthy and commendable.

Now, the simplicity of purpose here commended will practically gain these ends. It is the spirit and aim with which a thing is engaged in that gives character to the action. The *motive* is the great thing to be careful of. Herbert was right in his homely lines, already quoted:

> "Who sweeps a room as for thy laws
> Makes that and the action fine."

The legislator at the capital, the merchant on 'Change, the lawyer in the forum, the physician in the sick-room, the mother in the home circle, the trader in the warehouse, the porter under his burdens, the mechanic at his bench, the domestic at her service, ay, the scavenger at his street-cleaning,—may each render his or her business, in the best sense, a sacred pursuit by prosecuting it with the noble aim of benefiting others and pleasing God, and causing him to be honored on earth.

What is needful, then, is to bring the secular pursuits within the pale of religion. This is the grand and all-sufficient corrective; it is the desideratum of the times.

It would be impossible for the writer of these pages to convey to his readers the depth and earnestness of his desires, particularly that the young man of this day should adopt right views upon this great subject. He can only close with the entreaty that each reader will strive thus to live worthy of his great Original, and in keeping with his sublime destiny. How happy, not to say fruitful, will be such a life!

Socrates remarked, "that although pleasure and pain looked different ways, Jupiter had tied them together, so that he who lays hold on the one draws the other along with it." Here, as in other things, the great philosopher had need of being taught by him who is greater than he. Earthly pleasure and pain are mostly truly tied together, and he who takes hold of the one draws the other with it. But there is a pleasure to which pain is never attached. That is the pleasure of doing good. This pleasure hath no serpent's fangs in it, and it leaveth no sting behind.

The great Master has himself endorsed this, in declaring that "it is more blessed to give than to receive," and our own experience has often verified it, in the gratification that fills the bosom when we have befriended the friendless, fed the poor, clothed the naked, and soothed the anguish of some broken spirit. We have always found that "the dews of love which ascend from our soft pitying hearts fall back on them in showers of blessings." "*Dum vivimus, vivamus*," was the family motto of the excellent Dr. Doddridge. "While we live, let us live."

In his day, as now, this sentiment, perverted

and misapplied, was often adopted by the sensualist, and perhaps with a view to redeeming it from so base an application, Dr. Doddridge composed on the motto the following lines, pronounced by Dr. Johnson the finest epigram in the English language:

> "'Live while you live,' the epicure would say,
> 'And seize the pleasures of the present day!'
> 'Live while you live,' the sacred preacher cries,
> 'And give to God each moment as it flies.'
> Lord, in my view let both united be!
> I live in pleasure while I live to thee."

Here is truth couched in beauty. The sensualist, to attain happiness, puts the knife to the throat of virtue, and cutting loose from all restraints, eats, drinks, and is merry, believing, fool that he is, that a wicked disregard of God and his holy commandments secures enjoyment. But the truly wise man regards the matter as precisely the reverse of this. He, in order to be happy, loves his Maker, and tenaciously adheres to all his requirements. In his view happiness is married to virtue, and they twain cannot be put asunder.

Let me counsel the young upon a matter of such vast moment.

You desire happiness. Then listen to the voice which saith, "The liberal soul shall be made fat." "Give, and it shall be given unto you, good measure, pressed down, running over."

You desire happiness. The pursuit of the true objects of life yields that happiness, and not for this life alone, but for that which is to come. Our talents and energies, properly applied, make unto us friends who shall receive us into everlasting habitations when turned out of our present stewardship.

An old writer once said, "The riches which you export form the only wealth you will always retain;" and Bunyan's riddle runs thus:

> "A man there was, and some did count him mad,
> The more he cast away, the more he had."

If aught of earth shall heighten the joys of heaven, surely it shall be deeds of mercy, the remembrance of which outlasts the touch of death. How sweet shall be those pictures of memory! Blessed shall be that man who, by relieving want and soothing sorrow, has well hung the walls of heaven's mansions with such pictures!

IV.

SAYING "NO!"

"'Tis as easy to be heroes as to sit the idle slaves
Of a legendary virtue carved upon our fathers' graves."

AS Harry one day stepped into the country store, he heard the merchant reproving his boy for some wrong act, and was particularly struck with this remark: "My son, unless you learn to say 'No,' you are a ruined boy." He went away thinking of that item of parental counsel, and it is not too much to say that it did much to shape his whole life.

Upon a little reflection, the reader may recall persons who have suffered greatly, perhaps irreparably, simply because they could not say "No." What else brought the frown of God upon our first parents, and sin into the world with all its woes? It came from their not saying "No!" to the gilded words of the deceiver. What else brought shame and sorrow to King David in the case of Uriah and Bathsheba? Had he but said "No" to the suggestions of evil, he had been spared that terrible experience. What else—to come to the range of your own observation—ruined the fortunes of your good neighbor of a yielding disposition, when asked to put his name to that paper which obligated him to the amount of his property for another man's debt? His judgment disapproved of it as unsafe and unjust to his family; but he was urged and persuaded, he signed his name and was ruined! A simple "No" had prevented the calamity. And what else destroyed that promising youth whom you knew, whose career of vice was brought to so shameful an end? He was but the representative of a class. The case was plain. Had he but been able to utter this one little word, it had saved him. The history of a great many young men might be written thus (how many cases could you bring?): "He was too weak to resist; he was a good-hearted, generous fellow, but he lacked back-bone, stamina, firmness; he was easily led astray; he meant well enough, but, poor fellow, he never could say 'No!'"

Think a moment of the presence of temptation. It has pleased God to subject us to trial. We came into the world with a corrupt nature, drawing us downward when we ought to rise. Hence we must resist or be destroyed; and we no sooner step upon the threshold of responsible being than we meet the seductions of a corrupt world. These must be confronted and overcome, or we are ruined. Besides which, evil spirits exert a mysterious but actual and powerful influence upon us. With masterly art Satan seeks first to gain, then to hold, his victims. A grim fiend, he comes in disguised forms, and with words as musical as the whisperings of angels, and soft and insinuating as the dew drops descending upon the flowers. Here, too, is presented the alternative of resistance or ruin. We say, then, that temptations assail every one. It is impossible to escape them. They are within us and around us. A child may be shielded by the vigilance of parental love, and hemmed in and guarded by all the restraints of the purest and the best home on earth; but this will not bar the presence of evil. The time will come, sooner or later, when that child must encounter temptation. It will assail him where he is; and, then, homes do not last always; families are broken up, parents die, children grow up and leave the paternal roof, and the guarded youth reaches the time when he must act for himself. He is alone now, out in the world, and he must resist the approach of evil, or succumb to the power of the destroyer. In his experience there will be moments that will try him to the utmost, dangerous moments of awful but deceitful temptation to do wrong.

Let me specify some of these. Moments of peril come from the uprising of the passions. The passions are given to us for a wise purpose. They are the inward motive power, hurrying on the otherwise tardy train of feeling and action; but, like steam and fire and powder, while they are useful as servants, they are very bad masters. Alas, how often is their force destructive, because not properly restrained and directed! In our diseased moral constitutions there is danger of their acquiring a fearful supremacy. Where they do not, it is owing to a proper subjection and control. Here, then, you see room for decision. If you would make serviceable the passions in giving energy to lawful pursuits, and not allow them to concentrate in selfish or impure desire, setting on fire the whole course of nature, and consuming all that is beautiful and excellent within you, there must be resolution enough to utter a firm "No."

Evil associates constitute another trial. Almost any neighborhood has those who might be styled corrupters of the young, not intentionally, perhaps, and from design contaminating others, yet doing it as surely as they are brought into contact with them. Thus a knowing youth in a country school district may initiate others into the knowledge and practice of vice. Thus city-bred young men, adepts in wickedness, though pleasant and companionable, lead astray the unsuspecting. Who of all that I address is not in danger from this source? You may not have thought of it, but there is danger of suffering injury from those with whom you associate; one of those, perhaps, you consider your best friend. Here, too, you must say "No." Travelers have described how the broad arrowy Rhone, with its bright blue waters, darts from Lake Leman with the seeming joyousness of life, and is presently assailed by the turbid, boisterous Arve, which comes tearing down from the glaciers of Mont Blanc. The beautiful Rhone disdains the proffered union, and for a few miles the two rivers flow on side by side, the one all purity, the other all pollution, without mingling. The Arve, however, perseveres in its malign solicitations, until at length the noble stream consents to the fatal embrace and gradually exchanges its sparkling face for the foul hue of its destroyer. Picture of human fortunes without number! For a time the ingenuous and upright youth held himself aloof from the fascinations of vice, but the influence of companions was too strong and he yielded, surrendered his innocence and purity, and came to a dishonorable end.

Strong drink is a terrible temptation to many. If the arch enemy is to-day attacking the youth of our land, especially of our cities, at any one point more formidably than another, it is in inducing them to dally with intoxicating stimulants. It would seem that he had hoisted the very flood-gates of this vice, threatening to sweep away every barrier. I mention a case— merely a specimen example of the results of what is called a little harmless indulgence, mere dallying with drink. A young man stood gazing listlessly in at the windows of a pleasantly-lighted saloon one evening, when he felt a gentle tap on the shoulder. He turned, and a friend of his, taking his arm, said, "Come, I'm going in here a few moments; will you not come?" He hesitated; his mother rose before him as, on her dying bed, he promised her he never would sit at a gaming-table or look upon the wine-cup. But the tempter still urged. He entered. The first downward step was taken.

A few years passed away. Stretched on a bed is a poor, bloated, dying man, with frenzied eyes and writhing limbs. It is not necessary to follow him in the downward course of sin and misery. He had drank until he was struck with delirium tremens. Lying there he would point his attenuated finger toward the door and exclaim, "There they are! don't you see them? Oh, keep them off! There, they have got me! Yes, yes, I will play one more game with you, for you have my soul, I know you have. I will win it back." Thus he would rave, ever thinking he was playing with demons, that he might win back his soul, which he said they had got, until death palsied his arm and chilled his blood, when the strife was ended and the gambler and drunkard was no more. Oh, if he had but said "NO" when standing by that window!

Here is a case with different results. The junior class of a southern college had assembled in a student's room to spend the night in riot and debauch. Amid that crowd was one who had never recited a bad lesson since his matriculation. In his studies he was head and shoulders above his class. That day he had failed. A shade of deepest gloom came over him, and he was indescribably melancholy; but the wine and jest passed round, while himself felt like Lucifer in Eden, where all was joy and gladness around him. Said a classmate, "Come, Bob, quaff this bumper, and it will make you feel as bright as a hermit's lamp." The tempter whispered in his ear, "Drink once and forget the past. A similar occasion will never return." A powerful struggle seemed going on in his mind for a moment, but at last he silently shook his head, and retiring to the grove, gave vent to his feelings in a flood of tears. That boy never drank—not even once. He took the valedictory and is now president of a college. Oh, will not that man bless God to his latest day that he firmly met that temptation?

The following was a parley between two young men standing by a beer saloon:

"Come in, Joe, and let's take a drink."

"No, Thomas, I can't afford it."

"But, Joe, I'll pay for it."

"Oh, I am not speaking of loss of money, Thomas, but of loss of health and energy, moral principle, character, peace of mind, and self-respect."

This was sensible; and to emphasize it, read the terrible words of the amiable, brilliant, sociable, but dissipated Charles Lamb, whose remorse was only too late. He says:

"The waters have gone over me, but out of the black depths, could I be heard, I would cry out to all those who have but set a foot in the perilous flood. Could the youth to whom the flavor of his first wine is delicious, look into my desolation and be made to understand what a dreary thing it is when a man shall feel himself going down a precipice with open eyes and a passive will—to see his destruction and have no power to stop it, and yet feel it all the way emanating from himself—to see all godliness emptied out of him, and yet not able to forget a time when it was otherwise—to bear about the piteous spectacle of his own ruin—could he see my fevered eye, feverish from last night's drinking, and feverishly looking for to-night's repetition of the folly—could he but feel the body of the death out of which I cry hourly, with feebler outcry, to be delivered, it were enough to make him dash the sparkling beverage to the earth in all the pride of its mantling temptation."

Is not this enough to make you say "No"? Oh, if you would avoid the unutterable horrors of such an end, take warning before it is too late! Trust not to your ability to stop drinking when you please, but don't begin. Touch not, taste not, handle not; say "No."

Again, see a young man or woman entering upon city life. To throw an inexperienced, unsuspecting youth into a place of such concentrated iniquity must be a tremendous temptation. Is it surprising that one in four, the number alleged, of those who come to cities for a fortune turn out badly? What snares are spread for the feet! How liable to be entrapped! When during the late war new regiments were sent to the front, their pickets were often taken off in the following way: The enemy, approaching within thirty or forty rods of the outposts and concealing themselves in the woods, would commence the irregular tinkle of a cow-bell; the uninitiated picket, not suspecting the ruse and not yet reconciled to drinking his coffee without milk, goes out to obtain a supply, and not until he finds himself surrounded by a half dozen armed men does he discover his mistake. By some similar "cow-bell" dodge does the great adversary pick off many of the uninitiated who enter the city.

Is it your sister? Perhaps she is in a public boarding-house, where no unmarried woman ought to be except from sheer necessity, and the tinkling temptation is in the form of those adulatory remarks and seemingly kind attentions which men of libertinish character, who are apt to prowl about such houses, know how to use. Or perhaps as soon as she comes to the city she falls in the way of those ravening wolves whose accursed trade it is to give vice its victims. For that old legend of a monster, to satisfy whose voracious appetite a city had year by year to sacrifice a number of its virgins, who, amid the lamentations of their mothers and the grief of their kindred, were led away trembling to his bloody den, is no fable in cities.

Perhaps the new-comer is a young man, and the "dodge" is to get him to join a social club.

His excuse is that he wants some place to sit and read and talk and enjoy himself. But he wishes he had said "No," for he sees but too plainly that "club-rooms" are but another name for the devil's traps.

Or perhaps the special form of temptation is that depicted by a master hand in the Book of Proverbs, once for all time: "To deliver thee from the strange woman, even from the stranger which flattereth with her words; which forsaketh the guide of her youth, and forgetteth the covenant of her God; for her house inclineth unto death, and her paths unto the dead; none that go unto her returneth again, neither take they hold of the paths of life; for the lips of a strange woman drop as a honeycomb, and her mouth is smoother than oil; but her end is as bitter as wormwood, sharp as a two-edged sword; her feet go down to death, her steps take hold to hell; lest thou shouldest ponder the path of life her ways are movable, that thou canst not know them; hear me now, therefore, O ye children, and depart not from the words of my mouth; remove thy way far from her, and come not nigh the doors of her house; lest thou give thine honor unto others, and thy years unto the cruel; lest strangers be filled with thy wealth, and thy labors be in the house of a stranger; and thou mourn at the last, when thy flesh and thy body are consumed."

This leprosy has always cleaved to great cities, whose decay has been in all cases exactly measured by its prevalence.

But I need not specify. Let it suffice to say, that in great cities, while the restraints on vicious indulgence are few, the means of such indulgence are perilously accessible and inviting. The god of this world spreads here his richest banquets with the most seductive but poisoned viands. The very air seems tainted with the presence of specious lies, and pleasant sins, and lurking or open skepticism, and unblushing profanity, and filthy jesting, and mischievous influences of every conceivable kind.

It has been said that great cities are great sores. Babylon and Sodom and the cities of Judea became exceedingly corrupt. Of London, John Foster said, "If depravity, as an abstraction, could be clothed in a form which would render it perceptible by the eyes, the collective depravity of this magnificent city would be the most terrific and ominous apparition that man ever beheld;" and the same were true of any large city. In a few square miles evil enough often exists to poison a universe. As Cowper says:

> "Thither flow,
> As to a common and most noisome sewer,
> The dregs and feculence of every land.
> In cities, foul example, in most minds,
> Begets its likeness. Rank abundance breeds
> In gross and pampered cities, sloth and lust,
> And wantonness and gluttonous excess."

There is no form of sin or vice not found here, and in its most tempting display.

The reason for this is plain. It is not because individual depravity is greater in cities than in the country, but because it is centralized and organized. Firebrands go out if laid apart, but blaze if heaped together. A few specked apples on the tree do no harm, but barreled with others they rot the whole. In cities humanity is huddled, "barreled;" hence it is putrescent. Sin is rank, like weeds in a hot-bed. Burglars, swindlers, counterfeiters, inebriates, gamesters, villains of every stamp and hue, resort to cities; they meet here, and associate and keep each other in countenance, and so get strength. What is plainer than that a youth without firmness of soul to say, with David, "My heart is fixed," is sure to be destroyed?

Another temptation, addressed especially to young men, whether in city or country, is dishonesty. It is a sharp trial when a lad or youth comes first to handle money for his employer, and has free access to the money-drawer. Multitudes take their first decisive step downward by petty pilferings in this way. A clerk or apprentice boy has not all the money he wants; perhaps Satan whispers that more is honestly his due for what he does, and he finally thinks he will just take a little for a day or two, only borrowing it. But he finds it hard to repay it; then he despairs of doing it; then he concludes, if he has to steal, the disgrace being no more if found out, he will take twenty, thirty, fifty, instead of ten dollars, until he silences conscience, and goes on to positive and confirmed habits of thieving. From such small and seemingly excusable beginnings such fatal consequences flow, and the same is true of other forms of dishonesty, lying, deceiving, cheating, and the like. From the very thought of any dishonesty recoil with horror, uttering a firm "NO!"

Harry's Conflicts.

Page 127.

"Dare to be right! Dare to be true!
Other men's failures can never save you;
Stand by your conscience, your honor, your faith!
Stand like a hero, and battle till death!"

Then gaming, such as card-playing, lottery-dealing, raffling, betting, and the like, is often a temptation. The following incident, with its moral, is in point: Chaplain R—— was passing around among the soldiers, inviting them to a prayer-meeting. Stopping at a tent where several were playing cards, he said,

"You are too busy to come to prayer-meeting to-night?"

"Yes," answered a young man, self-confidently, "I am too busy; I am learning my first lesson at cards."

"Your first lesson!" said the chaplain. "Will you please give me your name?" taking out his memorandum-book.

"My name? No!" exclaimed the youth.

"Men," said the chaplain, in a firm tone of voice, "will you have the kindness to give me his name?"

"Oh, don't, don't!" he exclaimed, beseechingly.

"I want his name," continued the chaplain

seriously. "I may be called, one of these days, to preach his funeral sermon."

"Don't, don't!" vociferated the young man, hiding his face, so that the chaplain might not recognize him afterward.

The chaplain left, but the game of cards was spoiled for that night, and thus ended the first lesson. That young soldier stood outside the prayer-meeting a listener, and after this was a constant attendant.

Let every young man beware of his first lesson at cards. The recording angel will take down his name, and the fact will meet him at the judgment.

Discard all "chance" operations of every kind. If you do not, you are a gambler, a name which has in it a world of infamy and woe, and which writes the ruin of more men and more families than most imagine.

Theatrical amusements must also be named. If anything can be proved, this can, that the theatre is a corrupt institution. In the main— of course there are some exceptions—the actors and managers are persons of loose morals; nothing is plainer, the confessions of actors themselves admit it, and the slightest observation confirms it. The attendants, too, are, to a great extent, corrupt persons. Sir Walter Scott certainly would not represent the case more unfavorably than it deserved, and he says: "Unless in the case of strong attraction upon the stage, prostitutes and their admirers usually form the principal part of the audiences." A professed directory of vice, in doggerel verse, thus alludes to the gathering there of vile characters:

> "Like ants on mole hills, thither they repair:
> Like bees to hives, so numerously they throng
> It may be said to that place they belong."

In a sense it may be said they *belong* there. The theatre is the meeting-place of loose characters. There the depraved make the appointments of depraved vice; there speculators in wickedness, old traders and young traders in virtue, meet as on 'Change, and the prices current of virtue and vice are ascertained, and, in the various barterings of temptation, all virtues are exchanged for all vices. This is not speaking too strongly. History can no more lie than can figures, and the theatre has a history to which we may appeal. It dates back, eighteen hundred years and more, to the days of Greece and Rome. It has flourished in all ages since; and in all countries and times its character has been corrupting. He is either ignorant or dishonest that denies it, for solid facts affirm it. Pollock's lines are but just:

> "The theatre was from the very first
> The favorite haunt of sin, though honest men—
> Some very honest, wise, and worthy men—
> Maintained it might be turned to good account;
> And so perhaps it might, but never was.
> From first to last it was an evil place,
> And now such things are acted there as make
> The devils blush, and from the neighborhood
> Angels and holy men trembling retire."

But it is said, "Christians go to theatres;" then the more shame for them, and a saying of the ancients is quite in point: "A holy monk reproached the devil for stealing a young man of his charge at the theatre; to which Satan replied, 'I found him on my premises and took him.'"

As your friend, then, I entreat you to say "No" as to theatre-going. Go not once. "Only once" has brought many to shame. It breaks a resolve that you will not attend. It is going in the way of temptation, which is forbidden; and it may pave the way to go again. A young man said to a lady with whom he was walking one October evening in New York,

"Did you ever attend the theatre?"

The cheek of the lady crimsoned at the idea as she answered in the negative, and added,

"My mother has taught me from childhood that it was wrong to attend such places."

."But your mother formed improper prejudices from exaggerated accounts given by others; for I have often heard her say that she never attended one in her life;" and he spoke eloquently of the drama, tragedy, comedy, and dwelt with pathos on the important lessons which we there learn of human nature. "Go with me once," said he, "and judge for yourself."

Persuasion and curiosity triumphed over the maternal precept and example, as she hesitatingly replied, "I'll go *but* once." She went, and in that theatre a charm came over her like the one which the serpent sent forth from his dovelike eye. She went again and again, and from that house of mirth and laughter she was led to *that* house from whose portals she never returned. Young man, young woman, take the writer's advice on this subject, and one of these days you will thank him for it. Reject this advice, and that daughter's fate—only one of thousands—may be yours.

Now, how many motives conspire to urge you to make a firm resistance to these and all other temptations! The Bible teaches that the wicked do not live out half their days, and the testimony of observation is to the same effect.

But what is life worth to the vicious, even while it does last? Have you heard the story of the Italian artist who, meeting with a child of exquisite beauty, wished to preserve its features, for fear he should never see such loveliness again? So he painted the charming face upon canvas, and hung it upon the walls of his studio. In his most sombre hours that sweet, gentle countenance was like an angel of light to him. Its presence filled his soul with the purest aspirations. "If ever I find," he said, "a perfect contrast to this beauteous face, I will paint that also and hang them side by side, an ideal of heaven and hell." Years passed. At length, in a distant land, he saw in a prison which he visited the most hideous object he ever gazed upon—a fierce, haggard fiend, with glaring eyes and cheeks deeply furrowed with lust and crime.

The artist remembered his vow, and immediately painted a picture of this loathsome form to hang beside the portrait of the lovely boy. The contrast was perfect. His dream was realized. The two poles of the moral universe were before him. But what was the surprise of this artist, on inquiring into the history of the wretch, to find that he was once that very same lovely little boy! Both of these pictures, the angel and the demon, of the same soul, now hang side by side in a Tuscan gallery. Alas! it is not needful to travel to find such illustrations of the transforming powers of vice. Look at that brazen-faced, wanton-looking wreck of womanhood! Once she was a sweet, modest girl that blushed at the slightest indelicate allusion. See her now! Or look at that obese, bloated, brandy-burnt-visaged man! Once he was a joyous-hearted boy. What strange alchemy has wrought this bestial transformation? You know! And vice would transform *you* into just such a monster. Therefore say "*No!*"

On the other hand, consider the pleasure of overcoming temptation and keeping yourself pure. Good old John Bunyan says, "I have found a nest of honey in the carcass of the lion that roared upon me." So may you. Grapple with this lion of temptation whenever he roars upon you. Smite him down; leave him dead behind you; and then how sweet and precious your reward! Some time, if not to-day, its grateful remembrance shall be a nest of honey to you.

Moreover, consider the strength that comes from temptation resisted. Some savage tribes hold that the spirit of every enemy one slays enters into the slayer and becomes added to his own spirit, making him more a warrior. It is certainly true of the spiritual warfare. Every sin you slay brings an added strength to your character, making you a more brave and unconquerable warrior.

Consider again that herein is true heroism. There are a great many mistakes as to what is manly, or what makes a hero. Scripture settles the point. It teaches that he that masters *himself* is manly, is the true hero. Here is the record: "He that ruleth his own spirit is better than he that taketh a city." Why? Because he is a victor of a victor. And again: "He that hath no rule over his own spirit is like a city that is broken down and without walls."

He offers no resistance to a foe; he is no hero. Samson defeats the Philistines; but Delilah subdues him; and he that carried away the gates of Gaza sinks under the weight of his own sensuality. Therefore he that resists Delilah, and is not overcome by the senses, is greater than Samson. Hercules throttled monsters, but he did not throttle his own appetite; therefore he who does subdue his appetite is greater than Hercules. Many a man and woman, in bearing up courageously against some trial or temptation, is more heroic than was Cæsar or Alexander. Look at that young man surrounded by profanity and vulgarity, yet keeping clear of it; insulted for his religion, yet calmly bearing it; urged to drink or do some wrong thing, yet unyielding alike to persecutions or persuasions. He is a hero! That is being manly! Rightly did the earl of Sterline versify the case:

> "Who would the title of true worth were his
> Must vanquish vice, and no ill conceive:
> The bravest trophy ever man obtained
> Is that which o'er himself *himself* hath gained."

But how may one be enabled to say "No" effectually?

For one thing, habituate yourself to act from

a sense of duty; from the perception of what is right; from a desire to obey conscience and please God. So doing, you can scarcely fail to attain to a noble character.

Daniel Webster once had a party of friends dining with him at his residence in Marshfield. One of the number asked him, while seated at the table, what one thing had done most for him in his life; meaning thereby what one thing had contributed most to his success. Mr. Webster replied, "The most fruitful and elevating influence I have ever seemed to meet has been my impression of *obligation to God;*" and then he proceeded to discourse in the most eloquent manner upon the subject. Act thus; set the *Lord* always before you, and it will mightily help you to resist the approach of evil.

Take care of your thoughts. Evil thoughts, of selfish gratification, impurity, injustice, revenge, fraud, and the like, always go before evil deeds.

"Not yet wilt thou laugh with scoffers, not yet betray the innocent;
But if thou nourish in thy heart the revenge of injury or passion,
And travel in mortal haste the mazy labyrinths of guilt,

> Not long will crime be absent from the voice that doth
> invoke him to thy heart,
> And bitterly wilt thou grieve that these buds have ripened
> into poison."

"Keep thy heart with all diligence, for out of it are the issues of life;"—thence are the outgoings, the streams, that make up thy whole career.

Dally not with temptation. It is easy to say "No!" at the first, but very hard afterward. Little by little corruption comes. Intemperance comes from one cup of brandy or wine taken perhaps at a wedding, or New Year's call, or just to please a friend. Dishonesty comes from a little fraud, a small theft; profanity, from the use of one mild, half-profane expression; dissipation, from one visit to the ballroom or theatre; and open lewdness, from infrequent and carefully concealed vice. Oh, if through ignorance, forgetfulness, or want of resolution one of you has already begun the practice of some of these evils, summon courage and put an end to it now.

An English gentleman had a tame young lion which seemed to have become a lamb in gentleness, and was a favorite pet in moments of leisure. One day, falling asleep, his hand hung over the side of his couch. The lion came to his side and commenced licking the hand. Soon the file-like surface of the animal's tongue wore off the cuticle, and brought blood to the surface. The sleeper was disturbed, and moved his hand, when a growl startled him from his dreaming and half consciousness, to realize the terrible fact that the pet was a lion after all. With great self-possession, with the other hand he drew carefully from the pillow a revolver and shot his pet through the head. It was no trivial sacrifice to his feelings, but a moment's delay might have cost him his life. So do with any pet sin of yours. Spare it not, painful as it may be. Better cut off the right arm, or pluck out the right eye, than lose the soul in hell!

Be not influenced by the fear of man which bringeth a snare. Young people are very apt to be; they would be agreeable and companionable; they shudder at the thought of giving offence, of losing favor or caste, and especially of being ridiculed as Puritan, religious, green, rustic, stingy, unsociable, and the like. Here is a paragraph from Sidney Smith:

"Learn from your earliest days to inure your

principles against the peril of ridicule; you can no more exercise your reason, if you live in the constant dread of laughter, than you can enjoy your life if you are in the constant terror of death. If you think it right to differ from the times, and to make a point of morals, do it, however rustic, however antiquated, however pedantic, it may appear; do it, not for insolence, but seriously and grandly, as a man who wore a soul of his own in his bosom, and did not wait till it was breathed into him by the breath of fashion." Capital! act upon it, and no matter, no matter! "If sinners entice thee, consent thou not." Let your motto be, "Principle before approval," "death before dishonor," "duty before flattery," "verdant before rotten."

As a final direction, be a Christian. Little confidence can be placed in self-control without grace. It was the prayer of David, "Hold thou me up, and I shall be safe." We want God's Spirit in the soul to keep us. It was this that kept Joseph in his fearful temptation in Egypt, leading him to say "No; how can I do this great wickedness and sin against God?" Without this we are nothing but weakness. "I can do all things through Christ, which strengtheneth me," said Paul. Here is strength; nothing else is. Therefore be a Christian. Repent of sin; confess it; forsake it; trust in Jesus as a Saviour from sin; put your hand into the hand of the Almighty, saying, "Be thou, O Father, O Saviour, the guide of my youth." Ay,

> "Devote thyself to God, and thou wilt find
> He fights the battles of a will resigned.
> Love Jesus! Love will no base fear endure:
> Love Jesus, and of conquest rest secure."

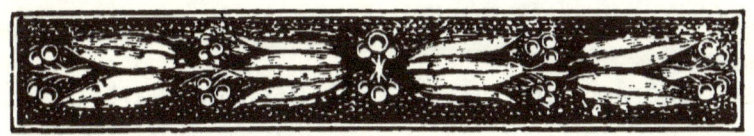

V.

HIGH AIMS.

"Rouse to some work of high and holy love,
  And thou an angel's happiness shalt know,
  Shalt bless the earth while in the world above:
  The good begun by thee shall onward flow
  In many a branching stream, and wider grow;
  The seed that in these few and fleeting hours
  Thy hands unsparing and unwearied sow
  Shall deck thy grave with amaranthine flowers,
And yield thee fruits divine in heaven's immortal bowers."

SOME one has written of Benjamin West, the celebrated painter, that a single word from his mother made him what he was. When a mere lad, he executed a rude and homely portrait of his infant sister. Upon showing it to his mother she commended him, and that word of encouragement set him upon the road to eminence.

Harry owed much to an idea which was deeply instilled into his mind by his mother—

so deeply, indeed, that it became part of his being. That idea was embodied in her injunction, "Aim to be somebody in the world." Among other plain utterances of hers on this point, she used to say, "If you aim at the moon in mid-heaven, you will shoot higher than if you aimed at the top of an apple tree." This idea is worthy of a little reflection.

The Scriptures nowhere discountenance self-respect, nor the desire to be respected by others. When one loses a respect for himself, his condition is indeed deplorable; he is already on the way to the lowest point of degradation; and unless one desires to enjoy the respect of others, he is nearly in the same condition. "I don't care what men think of me" is an ominous remark from any young man.

He who has really cast off all regard for the esteem of mankind has lost one of the most wholesome restraints from vice and an important stimulus to the practice of virtue.

I do not mean by this to minister to an unlawful ambition. The love of applause, or a thirst for honor, has been the ruin of not a few. Thousands in courting fame have been wedded to disgrace. In these instances a principle implanted in us by our Maker becomes perverted. That which was designed for good is abused and made the means of evil.

A wish to deserve well of our fellow-men is a virtue and not a vice. It is, however, like anger and many other passions, oftentimes sadly prostituted, and thus a virtuous principle becomes vicious. While, therefore, I would not be thought to commend a spirit of mere sordid ambition, and a time-serving policy to secure the honors or adulations of men, nor foster a desire to stand on the pinnacle of mere human glory, I would recommend that especially the young desire and seek to deserve the esteem and respect of all; that they imbibe such principles and lead such a life as to merit the honors bestowed on men of real worth. It is in this sense that I use the term honor. I accept Plutarch's definition. "True honor and distinction," says he, "consist in the sincere esteem and affection of the people, founded on real merit and effectual services." You should aim at this; it is commendable in every one to desire to be beloved, respected, and honored of mankind. He who desires it will seek to make himself worthy of it.

If you will analyze the character of the men who have filled a large place in the world's eye, you will find that it was some exalted purpose, some eminent point of attainment, that made them what they were. This was the case with Cæsar, who figured so largely in Roman history. During one of his journeys in Spain he came upon a statue of Alexander the Great that adorned an edifice in the city of the present Cadiz. He stood before that statue, and remembered that Alexander, though he died at the age of thirty, had made himself master of the world. He reflected also that he himself was already thirty-five, and that, though he had lived five years longer than Alexander, he was yet the second in a single province. He felt himself rebuked. His ambition was aroused, and he there became so fired with his zeal for glory that before his time expired he returned to Rome fully bent on acquiring power. It is probable that the standard of greatness which he then determined to reach, and which was as high as that to which Alexander himself had attained, more than anything else made Cæsar what he at length became. But for this elevated aim he might have ever remained but second in power, and that in a province.

Cicero might also be mentioned as illustrating our remark. One has doubtless testified truly of the secret of his greatness when he says, "It was that grand conception of eloquence which perpetually revolved in his mind, that idea of *aliquid immensum infinitumque*, of something immense and noble, which always haunted his thoughts and drew forth those splendid displays of genius which the world continues to admire but cannot rival."

The same was true of the Grecian orator. Had not Demosthenes aimed to be nothing less than Callistratus, by whose eloquence he was so entranced, he had not attained to his exalted eminence. Lord Nelson affirms that there was a time in his youthful days when he was on the point of yielding to despondency. "I felt impressed," said he, "with the thought that I should never rise in my profession. At length a sudden glow of patriotism was kindled in my bosom, and presented my king and my country as my patron. 'Well, then,' I exclaimed, 'I will be a hero!'" From that time a radiant orb, as he expressed it, was suspended before his mind's eye, which urged him on to honor and renown. Here was the secret of his greatness.

It is told of Thorwaldsen, the great Danish sculptor, that when found by a friend in a state of despondency, he pointed to his statue of Christ and exclaimed that his genius was decaying, as it was the first work he had ever felt satisfied with, nor should he again have a great idea, for he had reached his highest conception. He might well fear that his faculties were decaying. His "great idea" being wanting, he well knew he could no longer rise. Without a "great idea" many a bright name had never shone forth from the dim past.

> "Visions of an untold glory
> Milton saw in his eclipse;
>   *   *   *   *
> Holier Christs and veiled Madonnas
> Painted were on Raphael's soul;
> Melodies he could not utter
> O'er Beethoven's ear would roll."

When John C. Calhoun was in college, a classmate expressed his surprise that he should be found so ardently poring over "Malthus and Smith's Wealth of Nations," which he alleged would be of no use to him unless a member of

Congress, which station he could not expect to attain for the next twenty years.

"Twenty years! twenty years!" returned he. "Why, my friend, if I did not believe that before ten years have passed I should be in Congress, I pledge you my word I would leave college this moment." In eight years he was there. That lofty purpose, that high point of attainment, led him onward and upward.

That is a remarkable utterance in the writings of the apostle Paul where he declares that he has "not yet attained." At the time when he said it he was a man of the most elevated attainments—a man full of piety, full of years, full of trophies. Behold his benevolence, his readiness to sacrifice for the good of others. "I could wish that myself were accursed from Christ for my brethren." Behold his zeal. His spirit was "stirred within him," and he devoted himself, soul and body, a living sacrifice to God. Behold his courage. He withstood Peter to the face, and boldly rebuked arrogant power itself. Behold his disinterestedness. "We sought not glory of men, neither of you, nor yet of others." And then behold his record, to which he might have pointed. What unwearied toils! what hardships and sacrifices! "In journeyings often, in perils of waters, in perils of robbers, in perils by mine own countrymen, in perils by the heathen, in perils in the city, in perils in the wilderness, in perils in the sea, in perils among false brethren, in weariness and painfulness, in watching often, in hunger and thirst, in fastings often, in cold and nakedness." Moreover, what miracles had he wrought! what revelations had he experienced! what visions of unutterable glory in the third heaven, whither he had been caught up! Besides, what noted men and what nations had he brought over to the Christian faith, and how many churches had he founded and fostered into self-help!

Is this the man who utters the language, "Not yet attained"? Paul the apostle? The aged man? the aged Christian? the aged minister? the very man who could say, "I live; yet not I, but Christ liveth in me," who could say, "Who shall separate me from the love of God, which is in Christ Jesus my Lord?" and who could even say, "Brethren, be followers together of me, and mark them who walk so as ye have us for an example"?

Had you seen him then, just ripening off for

heaven, bending beneath the weight of age, within two years of the time of his departure, his countenance radiant with love, and the fire of heaven lighting up his eye, you would have said, "What evil passion remains in thy bosom, O thou devoted servant of the Lord Jesus? What conquest is yet to be made by thee, thou veteran of the cross? What greater thing yet remains for thee to compass, thou who shinest as the brightest star in Christ's hand, that thou shouldst say, 'I have not yet attained, I press toward the mark'?"

Yet this is his language; and herein—mark the point—was the mainspring of his rising; this was his striking characteristic. I know of no other passage in all his writings which so happily furnishes us with a key to his character and life. He was great because he meant to be greater still, because his aim was high, because he was reaching to something yet before.

We perceive, then, that it is an elevated aim which, under God, renders one truly great. This is true of Christians, statesmen, scholars, and all classes of men. Let me, therefore, urge upon you, my young friend, the importance of forming to yourself a high standard of excellence and real greatness. It is for want of this that thousands are almost cyphers in society; they never expect to be anything; they have no idea of rising higher than the mass of those around them, and, of course, remain on the same level. I would have you, instead of this, place before you characters of solid worth and distinction, and keep your eye on them until you are inspirited by their example, and impelled to press with earnestness to at least the point of eminence which they have attained. Let there be in your breast a commanding purpose, a fixed determination, to be truly great because of real attainments. I would not have my readers to be heroes, but men and women worthy of their noble natures and exalted privileges. The language of the venerable Dr. Nott, late president of the Union College, when once addressing his students, is much in point: "I have been young, and am now old, and, in review of the past and the prospect of the future, I declare unto you, beloved pupils, were it permitted me to live my life over again, I would from the very outset live better—yes, from the very outset, I would frown upon vice, I would favor virtue, and lend my influence to advance whatever would exalt and adorn human nature, alleviate human misery, and contribute to render the world I live in, like the heaven to which I aspire, the abode of innocence and felicity; yes, though I were to exist no longer than the ephemera that sport away their hour in the sunbeams of the morning, even during that brief period I would rather soar with the eagle, and leave the record of my flight and fall among the stars, than creep the earth and lick the dust with the reptile, and having done so, bed my body with my memory in the gutter."

And let me say that the young of this age should aim at greater things than their fathers accomplished, because their opportunities are greater. Enterprise has established communication the world over, so that the nations are next-door neighbors. The languages of all countries have been reduced to writing; the Scriptures are translated into every tongue, and mission stations, like dim and distant watchfires upon the mountains, are beginning to sparkle over vast fields of hitherto unbroken darkness. Meanwhile, the breath of the Almighty seems to have passed over all flesh, awakening it to unprecedented animation. Apathy is gone, investigation is alive, conscience is on edge, and errorists are rousing as to a last battle. Casting the eye over the world, and regarding even the most unpromising parts of it, it does appear "white and ready for the harvest." How ought the youth of to-day to thank God for their great opportunities, and to undertake and expect great things! Be your resolve, young friend, in keeping with this sentiment; without this lofty purpose, this firm determination to do something and be somebody because of a well-spent life, you may abandon the hope of real greatness, and be content with the expectation of being but little known and esteemed in life, and soon forgotten when life shall end.

Moreover, pursue this end with a steady aim. It has been well said that a man's purpose of life should be like a river which was born of a thousand little rills in the mountains, and when at last it has reached its manhood in the plain— though, if you watch it, you shall see little eddies that seemed as if they had changed their minds and were going back again to the mountains—yet all its mighty current flows changeless to the sea. If you build a dam across it, in a few hours it will go over it with a voice of victory. If tides check it at its mouth, it is only that when they ebb it can sweep on again to the ocean. So goes the Amazon or the Orinoco across a continent, never losing its way or changing its direction for the thousand streams that fall into it on the right hand and on the left, but only using them to increase its force, and bearing them onward in its resistless channel.

Another essential prerequisite is decision of character or fixedness of principles.

For want of this whole multitudes are ruined. No one destitute of it can attain to eminence. The world is full of temptations, and the flesh and the great enemy of mankind are leagued to render man belittled and besotted by causing him to indulge in practices forbidden alike by the word of God and the laws of our nature.

Hence the need of cultivating established rules or principles of life from which we will not depart. It was this which saved Joseph in Egypt when tempted by an infamous character to do evil. He replied, Nay, how can I do this wicked thing? and fled as for his life from the tempter. But for this he had not reached the glory to which he was afterward exalted. It was decision of character, too, that makes the name of Daniel so illustrious in the holy writings. Though in the very hotbed of vice and in a heathen land, though threatened with death in a den of lions, he swerved not an hair's breadth from the rule of duty he had resolved to follow. He still entered his house, raised his window toward Jerusalem and prayed, as always, three times a day, though forbidden to pray to the King of heaven. God delivered him not only, but both God and men, even his enemies, honored him. You will find this same firmness of character necessary oftentimes in life, and for want of it you may have already suffered much injury.

My advice, then, is, Go to the word of God and learn what is right, what is duty, what are the laws of God which govern us; and when you have ascertained them, abide by them with an undying determination. Do what is right, let the consequences be what they may.

Of what worth in society is the man destitute of this decision of purpose and character? He is driven about by every wind that may chance to blow. He is unfit for business: he cannot succeed in it because too vacillating; he is unfit for service in his country's cause: he cannot be depended upon; and besides this, he is so much the sport of circumstances, the easy prey of every tempter, that he is not, nor can he be, himself happy and contented. He is a poor, imbecile, pitiable, contemptible creature, and all because he has not firmness of principle. Let him serve at least one good purpose, to admonish and warn you of such fatal indecision.

I would advise you to read Foster on Decision of Character, and other works of like nature, as a means of incitement and instruction in acquiring this feature of character. Without this, depend upon it, you will live to little purpose; your attainments will be at best but moderate, and even these may not save you from infamy. Let your ways, then, be established. Heed the admonition of one of years and experience: "The wind and waves may beat against a rock planted in a troubled sea, but it remains unmoved. Be you like that rock, ye young! Vice may entice, and the song and the cup may invite. Beware! stand firmly at your post. Let your principles shine forth unobscured. There is glory in the thought that you have resisted temptation and overcome."

I have no hope of eminence in attainments on

the part of any unstable, double-minded, unprincipled youth. A hundred chances to one that he will make shipwreck somewhere in his passage o'er the treacherous sea of life. But present to me one of fixed principles of action, of unbending purpose to adhere to such rules of life as wisdom dictates, one

> "Who does as reason, not as fancy, bids,
> Who hears temptation sing and yet turns not
> Aside; sees sin bedeck her flowery bed,
> And yet will not go up; feels at his heart
> The sword unsheathed, yet will not sell the truth;
> Who, finally, in strong integrity
> Of soul, 'midst want or riches or disgrace
> Uplifted calmly sits, and hears the waves
> Of stormy folly breaking at his feet,"—

show me such a one, and you have found the youth that will yet be honored and esteemed, be his condition now what it may.

Industry is another condition to true honor.

There is a sad misconception, which is sometimes entertained by the young, that it is degrading to labor, that it is inconsistent with a life of gentility and refinement to have any particular employment at which they are found working, that it is disgraceful to bear the marks of hardy toil. Such sentiments are too common. We may well sigh for the simplicity of ancient times, when a Rebecca and a Rachel, a David and a Paul, wrought with their own hands; when a Homer could sing of princesses who drew forth water from the springs and washed the linen of their respected families; when the greatest monarch and conqueror the world ever saw, and daughters of the most remarkable queen known in other days made with their own fingers the garments with which their brother, the world's conqueror, was attired, and when princesses themselves thought it no ignominy to descend from the throne and assist in domestic duties.

Alas that it is no longer the eulogy of woman that "she layeth her hands to the spindle and her hands hold the distaff," that she "looketh well to the ways of her household and eateth not the bread of idleness," and that it has become disreputable in the esteem of some to live in keeping with the inspired injunction, "This we command you, that if any should not work neither should he eat," and that "with quietness they work and eat their own bread." It is well, however, that a correct sentiment upon this subject prevails so generally as it does, and that industry is being more and more honored by the great and good.

An active life of some kind leads to honor, because it is necessary to the full development of one's mental and physical energies, and there must be some leading, commanding object of interest, to arouse, stimulate, and ennoble the powers of man. I can heartily endorse the language of one who said, " I would rather have a child of mine begin life with nothing to rely upon but his own exertions than be the heir to the richest estate in the country. Character and success depend vastly more on personal effort than any external advantages. With such efforts the humblest cannot fail to rise; without such efforts the highest cannot fail to sink."

Besides, industry is desirable, if for no other reason than to prevent from vice. Isaac Watts never sang truer lines than these:

> " And Satan finds some mischief still
> For idle hands to do."

Vice is almost the sure concomitant of idleness. If one does not find himself something to do, the devil will. The historian tells us, speaking of Alexander's excesses, " He wanted action and motion, for he always, when unemployed, lost part of the glory he had acquired in war." The record of the life of this wholesale murderer proves it, and verifies the remark that "the rust of idleness is far more destructive both to body and soul than the friction of the most intense activity."

Would you, therefore, young friend, attain to respectability and usefulness in life, be industrious, whatever your circumstances or prospects as to wealth. Avoid idleness as the canker of worth and the badge of disgrace.

I remark again that habits of morality are necessary to the attainment of true honor. It is—I am happy to make such a remark—it is becoming more and more necessary that he who is to be promoted respects the Bible and our holy religion, and at least externally conforms to its dictates. One of our earliest Presidents, Jefferson, said, "Were I to commence my administration again with the experience I now have, the first question I would ask respecting a candidate would be, Does he use intoxicating drinks?" So highly did he value correct morals in this respect. It is related that Nicholas Biddle, Esq., once president of the Bank of the

United States, that he dismissed a clerk because he refused to write for him on the Lord's Day. The young man, with a mother dependent on his exertions, was thus thrown out of employment by what some would call an over-nice conscience. A few days after this, Mr. Biddle, being requested to nominate a cashier for another bank, recommended this very young man, and mentioned this incident as proof of his trustworthiness. "You can trust him," said he, "for he would not work for me on Sunday." Here you perceive how a man is compelled to respect correct morals, even though he does not practice them, and how sure of honor is one who does what is right.

I entreat of you then, young friend, cultivate correct morals if from no higher motive than that here presented.

> "The low desire, the base design,
>   That makes another's virtues less;
> The revel of the giddy wine,
>   And all occasions of excess,
>
> "All thoughts of ill; all evil deeds
>   That have their root in thought of ill,
> Whatever hinders or impedes
>   The action of the nobler will,—

> "All these must first be trampled down
> Beneath our feet if we would gain,
> In the bright fields of fair renown,
> The right of eminent domain."

Be strictly honest. Some of you have the opportunity, and are tempted perhaps to take, it may be, money from the drawer of your employers—it is a desperate temptation, and ruins thousands—or in some way to possess yourself of that to which you are not entitled; and hereafter, when you are acting for yourselves, by unjust charges or unfair dealing you will be tempted to take the advantage of others. But forget never that honesty is, on all accounts, "the best policy." "Riches got by deceit," it has been said, "cheat no man so much as the getter; riches bought with guile God will pay for with vengeance; riches got by fraud are dug out of one's own heart, and destroy the mine."

Live or die, fall or rise, be honest; if you cannot succeed in business and be so, then leave your business; if you cannot be honest where you are, then change your position or employment. By no means be dishonest.

Many years ago there was a lad in Ireland

who was put to work in a linen factory, and while at work there was a piece of cloth that wanted to be sent out which was short of the quantity, but the master thought that it might be made the length by stretching a little; he unrolled the cloth, taking hold of one end of it himself and the boy at the other. He then said, "Pull, Adam, pull!" The boy said, "I can't." "Why not?" said the master. "Because it is wrong." Upon this the master said he would not do for a linen manufacturer; but that boy became Dr. Adam Clarke.

It is always safe to be right, because God is on the side of the right. "If God be for us who can be against us?" When Antigonus was ready to engage in a sea-fight with Ptolemy's armada, and the pilot cried out, "How many more they are than we!" the courageous king replied, "'Tis true, if you count their numbers; but for how many do you value ME?" One God is sufficient against all the combined forces of earth and hell.

Cultivate also an unflinching integrity. Speak the truth, though it be apparently at the greatest sacrifice. Under no circumstances whatever swerve a hair's breadth from the exact truth.

"Dare to be true; nothing can need a lie:
The fault that needs it most grows tired thereby."

I admire the boldness of that Reformer who, when some one said to him, "The world is against you," calmly replied, "Then I am against the world!"

Again, would you attain to true honor, be useful; serve the generation in which you live, and live for generations yet to come; in other words, self-sacrifice is a prerequisite to true honor. If you serve your fellow-men, they will honor you; a life of real usefulness is always one of respect, even in the eyes of the worst of men. More than this, in loving and doing good to your race God will honor you. Doing it with right motives is serving God, and the Lord has said, "If any man serve me, him will my Father honor," and again it is said, "The righteous shall be in everlasting remembrance."

The orderings of God's providence are a striking commentary upon this doctrine. It so occurs in the providence of God that those who are the most strictly benefactors and the servants of their fellows are pronounced by the world great. It may not be so while they are living—the award may be delayed; but generally at last, when a man's deeds become matters of history, benefactors only are the honored and the praised.

This is a most striking fact. Men may for a time shine and dazzle in a career of selfish ambition, but in the end they find their level, and their names either sink into oblivion or are known but to be held in contempt. To illustrate this remark, who cares now for the kings and nobles of the ancient provinces of the East, Egypt, Persia, Assyria? Whose heart warms as he reads over the names of the ambitious conquerors in Roman and Grecian history, or of any of the thousands of the grand and the titled of other countries and days? Who cares for them? But there are those whom the world will not let die; and who are they? It is easily told. They are just those who displayed unwonted patriotism and benevolence; those who trampled down despots or broke the chain of tyranny; those who forgot self-interest; those who threw themselves into the breach, and allied themselves to the wronged and the suffering, or who, in some especial way, devoted their time and talents to the good of others, relieving their distress and opening up to them new sources of enjoyment; in a word, they are those who were the servants of their fellows. These are the names which are shrined in the hearts and woven in the songs and benedictions of generations without end.

And observe that they are honored and beloved just in proportion as they were the public servants. The lower they descended, the nearer they approximated to the servant of all, especially the poor and the wretched and the forsaken, becoming, as it were, a servant of servants, the higher do they now stand in the esteem of their successors. Do you doubt it? Witness Howard the philanthropist, who devoted himself with an almost unparalleled abandonment to the relief of paupers and criminals in the most loathsome and infectious dungeons and lazarettoes; and Wilberforce; and Washington, the father of his country, at the mention of whose name the heart of every American bounds within him; and, in these our times, Florence Nightingale, turning into an angel of mercy, and following in the track of a distant and desolating war, soothing the dying and ministering to the sick and wounded, and whose very shadow the poor soldiers kissed as she passed by, and who sits to-day queen in Britain's affections next to her who sits queen on the throne; and a Havelock abandoning the charms of home at his country's call, and literally dying in his country's cause, and whose name is a legacy throughout the civilized world; and that gallant sea-captain who, when his ship was sinking, refused to enter the life-boat, and stood to his post, helping others till enveloped in the waters, and who from obscurity became the admiration of all who read the sad recital; and that young preacher in one of our cities who for his noble stand for the right was ejected from his pulpit, and banished from the society and the homes where before he was an idol, but who suddenly became great, and whose "stand up for Jesus" will remain, as now, a watchword and a remembrance in the days to come. Numerous other examples might be mentioned.

Were you to tell how these individuals came to such eminence, you could not better answer than by saying: "They acted, though unconsciously, on the principle announced by the great Teacher, that 'whosoever will be chief must become the servant of all.'" They came to be "chief" by their self-forgetfulness and devotion to the interests of others. So true is it that in the orderings of Providence the palm of real greatness is sure, sooner or later, to be awarded to those who serve their generation by the will of God.

I hope that no one of my readers will imagine that this real greatness cannot be attained on account of limited means or circumstances, or while moving in the humble walks of life. Our motives may be just as pure, our aim just as high, our lives just as truly great in God's sight, if laboring on the farm, or in the shop, or being occupied with the cares of the family, as in becoming ministers or missionaries. A right aim sanctifies all. If the eye be single, the whole body is full of light. It has been truly said that the cobbler can consecrate his lapstone, while many a minister has desecrated his pulpit. The ploughman can put his hand to the plough in as holy a manner as ever did minister to the sacramental bread. In dealing with your ribbons and your groceries, in handling your bricks and your jack-planes, you can be as truly priests to God as were those who slew the bullocks and burned them with the holy fire in the days of yore.

In a bookstore in New York may be seen a

picture of the great dissenters of the Scottish church struggle, as they are in council planning the mighty Free Church movement. How prominent a part Dr. Thomas Chalmers took in that movement is well known. But he not more excites my admiration, as seen in that splendid intellectual arena, than in the quiet sphere of his daily pastoral work, where, in one instance, he was found in the garret of a poor family bending over the stove and sprinkling oatmeal into the kettle, to make some gruel to feed the sick mother and her hungry children.

Alas that true greatness is so poorly understood! Man's idea of greatness is to get upon the shoulders of others. God's idea of greatness is to get our shoulders under others! We think that to be a king is to be great. Christ says that to be servant is to be great. The highest place of honor, in God's sight, is the lowest place of service. Stooping, not soaring, is the way to distinction in his kingdom. To carry, not to be carried, is honorable.

And who may not thus do something directly to serve his generation by the will of God, even though immersed in secular pursuits? Thomas Cranfield was a tailor, yet he labored among the bricklayers, in Sunday- and infant-schools, and other good works. John Pounds was a cobbler, yet he became the founder of ragged schools. Harlan Page was a joiner, but out of one hundred and twenty-five of his Sunday-school scholars at one time eighty-four gave evidences of true piety, and six became preachers of the gospel. Of one hundred young women employed in the Tract and Bible houses, sixty were brought to Christ, besides many others he heard not of. Sheets of the word of God, and tracts, as they were folded and stitched, were seen to be moistened with the tears from broken hearts, but who were doubtless saved eternally through his instrumentality. Sarah Martin was the dressmaker at Yarmouth, yet the kind missionary in the workhouses and in the jail. Thomas Dakin was the humble Greenwich pensioner and tract distributor; but for nearly twenty years he frequently distributed one hundred and fifty thousand a year. Clarkson, Wilberforce, and Buxton were statesmen. The Thorntons were merchants. David Nasmith was a clerk in Glasgow, yet the founder of city missions in Scotland, Ireland, America, Paris, London, and also the originator of the Monthly Tract Society,

Female Mission, and other benevolent institutions.

No matter, then, what your sphere of life is, begin when young to be useful, seeking out ways in which you may do good, and make it the great object of life to exalt and bless your fellow-man.

Of Sir Christopher Wren it is inscribed in St. Paul's, in London, "Si monumentum requiris circumspice"—"If you inquire for his monument, look about you." Aspire to even a better inscription at your departure. Leave everywhere about you the imperishable monuments of your usefulness.

"God is building here a temple,
   Day by day its walls arise;
He hath laid a sure foundation,
   And its top shall reach the skies.
Every good deed, howe'er humble,
   In the structure finds a place,
And the mighty Master-builder
   Fashions all with heavenly grace.

"Hast thou raised a prostrate brother?
   Hast thou saved a soul from sin?
Though unknown, despised, forgotten,
   May thy work of love have been,

God has wrought it in the temple,
   It is whiter than the snow,
Brighter than the flashing ruby,
   Purer than the diamond's glow.

"Time hath now no power to mar it;
   'Tis immortal as thy soul;
It shall be a thing of beauty,
   While eternal ages roll.
When the mighty walls are finished,
   And the temple is complete,
It shall be for a trophy,
   Making all thy joy more sweet."

In order to compass this end of a useful life, accustom yourself to be covetous of the intervals and fragments of time which so many waste. When Madame de Genlis was a companion of the queen of France, it was her duty to be at the table and waiting for her mistress fifteen minutes before dinner. These fifteen minutes were faithfully improved each day, and a volume or two was the result.

A writer of the present day, whose power is felt, says of himself, "Very nearly all that I have ever attained or done out of the regular routine of my professional duties has been by taking up those odd moments which are so easily thrown away."

Alfred the Great, one of the brightest lights of history, performed an amount of labor that was truly amazing. The affairs of his kingdom were so complicated as to require the wisest legislation and a personal inspection of each province of his dominions; but so carefully did he husband his time that he was able to apply himself vigorously to literary pursuits, and produced twenty original and translated books: and with all this he devoted eight hours out of the twenty-four to devotional exercises.

Luther, amid all his travels and active labors, besides other literary labors, prepared a translation of the whole Bible; and this was accomplished by doing something every day, and allowing no interval of time to pass unimproved.

John Wesley was a pattern of labor and industry. He traveled about five thousand miles every year, preached three times a day, rose at five in the morning, and his published works number nearly two hundred volumes.

Elihu Burritt, "the learned blacksmith," by persevering study in the intervals of labor, became one of the most distinguished linguists of any age.

It is related of Daniel Webster, "the intellectual giant of his generation," that, while he assisted his father at the saw-mill where he worked, he always carried with him some favorite author; and while waiting for the saw to pass through the logs, which occupied about ten minutes, he employed those brief intervals by eagerly devouring the contents of the volumes, and, in the last year of his life, he was able to repeat large portions of the books with which he had become familiar in this manner.

This leads to the remark that mental culture and the acquisition of knowledge are a means to accomplish high aims.

One of the old artists was thus interrogated by a tyro whom he was teaching to paint:

"Pray, master, how do you mix your colors?"

"With brains," was the reply.

It was a capital answer. A man of brains has always the advantage of one without them, no matter what the pursuit. To-day it is not capital that is wanted half so much as it is brain. Everywhere this pays well. A man who does a thing in a bungling way, who is a dolt, can hardly expect to succeed in this intelligent age. You cannot successfully match muscle against mind. Nor can you trust to "good luck." The only way to be sure of success, under God, is to deserve it, to compel it by the possession of sheer merit. Young friend, get brains. It is a good article to mix with almost anything.

But far more important than all else, if one would attain eminence and deserve well of his age, is piety. The way to live truly for this world is to forget self and live for the next world. You must sink before you rise. You must go down before you go up. You must die before you live. You must become nothing that so God may make you something. You must oppose self, and crucify self, and forsake self, and go out in longing affection toward God, before he will honor you and own you as a dear child.

Thus ally yourself to deity, thus aim, thus live; and though your departure hence be even in youth, yours shall have been a noble and honored career. Years do not make up life. A short life may yet be a long one, measured by what it accomplished. And a long life may be no life at all. Mere existence is not life. Deeds make life.

" 'Tis not the number of the lines on life's fast-filling page,
'Tis not the pulse's added throbs, which constitute our age.

Some souls are serfs among the free, while others nobly
 thrive;
Some stand just where their fathers stood—dead, even while
 they live;
Others, all spirit, heart, and sense, theirs the mysterious
 power
To live, in thrills of joy or woe, a twelvemonth in an hour!
Seize, then, the minutes as they pass; the woof of life is
 thought;
Warm up the colors, let them glow, by fire or fancy fraught.
Live to some purpose; make thy life a gift of use to thee,
A joy, a good, a golden hope, a heavenly argosy!"

VI.

THE INNER NEED.

> "I heard the voice of Jesus say,
>   'Come unto me and rest;
> Lay down, thou weary one, lay down
>   Thy head upon my breast.'
> I came to Jesus as I was,
>   Weary, and worn, and sad;
> I found in him a resting-place,
>   And he has made me glad."

MAN is not all body, nor is this life his whole existence. Yet how few seriously ask, "What am I? Whence am I? Who sent me here? For what am I here? Where am I at last to go?"

Nothing is so much neglected as the most valuable part. We are quick to answer the demands of the body, but too few seem even to know that they have soul-wants. The immortal nature within! Alas! it is left uncared for, unclothed, unfed, unblest.

But what is the great want of the soul? It is easily told. Its one great, all-comprehensive need is Jesus Christ. I think this can be made plain to any ordinary mind. If we consider carefully, we shall find that man, as an immortal and accountable being, needs three things, and but three. These are light and expiation and a conscious union with God which secures his help and salvation. Let us take them up in their order, and see how Christ meets these several wants.

Man's first great want is light, or knowledge—a knowledge of his origin and duty, and particularly of his destiny.

"What will become of me when I die?" said a thoughtful Hindoo as he lay upon his death couch.

"Oh," said the Brahmin who stood by, "you will inhabit another body."

"And where," said he, "shall I go then?"

"Into another."

"And where then?"

"Into another, and so on through thousands of millions of years."

Darting across that whole period, he cried out, "Where shall I go then?" and paganism could not answer. The last deep, agonizing cry was, "Where shall I go last of all?" and with these words he plunged into the vast unknown.

Now, that pagan but showed what is in your own breast. You know that you will live always; deny it though you may, you believe it still—you must believe it—and you cannot be indifferent as to the destiny before you. In the most careless moments you cannot be wholly so; and when you come seriously to reflect, this question of certainty as to the hereafter pains your soul. Says Dr. Mason, a missionary to the Karens, "The first earnest prayer I ever offered was, 'Lord, I am in darkness: grant me light!'"

Now, see how Christ meets this great want of our nature. As "the Light of the world," a "Light to lighten the Gentiles," he comes to substitute certainty for uncertainty. He finds a man busied with the problem of his own origin and nature and true end, and he reveals himself to himself. He finds one prying into the being and attribute of God, and he "shows unto us the Father." He finds him anxious as to the "chief good," and he reveals himself as the chief good. He finds a man shuddering on the verge of the tomb, and, like the Roman emperor Hadrian, asking of the vital principle within, "Poor fluttering, lively spirit, poor guest and comrade of the body, to what unknown regions wilt thou wing thy way, pale, naked, trembling?" or, like the dying Hindoo, inquiring, "Where shall I go then?" and he dissipates impending night, pouring a flood of light upon the grave and the dread hereafter.

The next want of the soul is conscious expiation. As just intimated, man admits his guilt, even though he may deny it, and he would pacify the known or unknown God by purging away sin. Hence the religious susceptibility of men everywhere, and the religious rites of the unenlightened. "Whether true or false," says the historian Thiers, "sublime or ridiculous, man must have religion. Everywhere we find him worshiping at some shrine, in all ages, in all countries." And the aim of all is expiation. Every ancient form of rude religious service; every costly temple reared for heathen worship; every living body burned upon the funeral pile, or crushed beneath the wheels of the idol car; every ablution in sacred waters; every maiden decking some idol shrine with sweet summer flowers; every mother casting her darling child into the mouth of the crocodile or into the fire,—is but the outward manifestation of a felt desire for propitiation and freedom from sin. It is but a blind groping after Christ and the blood of his atonement.

If you consult your own nature, you admit this same necessity of expiation. You know that you are not fit to meet God. At times it troubles you. If not to-day, yet when the Holy Spirit opens your eyes to behold the depth and fearfulness of your guilt, you will feel and acknowledge that sin must be got rid of!

Now, just this is gained through our Lord Jesus Christ. He came to destroy this work of the devil, to bear away the sin of the world. To the myriads in lands remote who vainly seek to gain this end by bleeding victims, and self-laceration, and toilsome pilgrimage, he, the Lamb of God, presents instead the one sacrifice of himself on the cross. And to the convicted sinner in Christian lands, how suited is Christ! He alone can help in this extremity. He alone can say, "Look unto me and live; thirsting, famishing, dying sinner, come unto me and drink." Thank God, he can say it, he does say it! God has exalted him to give repentance and remission of sins. His blood, oh, his blood! it has power to cleanse away the deepest stain. It speaketh better things than that of Abel. It cries not for vengeance, but for mercy and forgiveness. It brings peace, and comfort, and joy in the Holy Ghost.

The other great soul-need of man is to get back to his lost Father and be reinstated in his favor. The soul is of heavenly origin; and though sundered from God by sin, there is a conscious or unconscious longing for its primeval centre-point and resting-place. An amputated limb, it is said, seems to vibrate toward the part that is lost. The separated nerves appear to be in pain for their former connection. So the pulsations and throbbings of the soul are toward God, from whom it is now "far off by wicked works." The desire for inward repose, as we call it—peace, tranquillity of spirit, rest—what is it but this instinctive feeling after God? And how apparent along the whole line of history! As Dr. Schaff has beautifully said in his History of the Apostolic Church, "Through the dark labyrinth of mythological tales and traditions it is easy to trace the golden thread of this deep desire for reunion with God. The story of the prodigal son who wandered away from his father's house, but retained, even in his lowest degradation, a painful remembrance of his native home, is a true picture of the heathen world." "All the scattered elements of truth and beauty and virtue," says an historical writer, "in the religion, science, and art of ancient Greece and Rome, we must consider, with Tertullian, as the testimonies of a soul leaning in its deepest instincts and noblest desires toward Christianity, and predestined for it as the fulfillment of its wants and its hopes."

Man was made for God, designed to be his companion; hence his heart is restless till it finds God. Disturbed by the presence of sin, yet with tremulous motion it sweeps to and fro,

"'True as the needle to the northern pole,"

nor rests till it comes into range with the great heart of the universe. This as nothing else can explains to you that ineffable yearning of the heart after some unrealized good which your deeper consciousness reveals; that listening of the upturned ear of your soul to catch the feeble cadences of some half-remembered celestial harmony; that reaching out of your unblest being after something upon which it may lean and steady and rest itself.

Now, see how Christ meets this acknowledged want. Did he not come to bring us back to God? Is he not the Restorer of fallen humanity? and, as such, was he not the " desire of all nations," the object looked for and longed for, the centre alike of the world's history and of the individual heart? In him the God-man, the divine and the human, were strangely conjoined. He was God, and at the same time man. Oh, wondrous union! He stepped in as our Daysman, and laid his hands upon us both, the offender and the offended; he spanned the yawning chasm opened by the shock of the fall, and put us once more, through himself, into communication with our Maker and God. And for what lives he now but to perfect this reunion in individual experience?—but to take, as it were, in his own hands, the bleeding ligaments of our dissevered hearts, and attach them to the great heart of the Eternal? And oh, when by faith this sundered tie is thus reunited, as the branch to the vine, then how vitality and health do pour through all the delighted sensibilities! How the agitations of the soul die away! how heart beats responsive to heart! how the peace of God, which passeth all understanding, comes to be enjoyed! Rightly said old Augustine, "Lord, thou hast made man for thee, and our heart cannot rest until it come to thee." Vain the trial, fruitless the effort, to get repose in any other way; it has been tried ever since the world begun, and failed every time. No, no! history utters it; the human bosom utters it; the page of inspiration utters it. Strangers to God, we are strangers to bliss.

Take note, then, of the sources of your uneasiness, my friend. "*I want Christ!*" This is the interpretation of that sigh and that search of yours. It is the same old cry of the ages; the ever-reappearing refrain in all the utterances of the past; the real underbeat in the still sad music of universal humanity.

There was a time, as we have previously seen, in Harry's experience, when he awoke to these necessities of his spiritual part, and most happily did he find them all met in his blessed Lord. If you, my dear friend, are not yet conscious of these soul-wants, is it not because you have failed to give them proper consideration? Will you not allow them now, at least for a few moments, to occupy your mind?

You must admit that you are not fully happy; that with all your pleasant surroundings, your cheerful disposition, and your bright hopes there is still an aching void, a something unsupplied, which forbids ease and solid satisfaction. A French physician was once consulted by a person who represented himself as subject to the most gloomy fits of melancholy. The physician advised his patient to visit scenes of gayety, and particularly the Italian theatre, and added,

"If Carlini [a famous comic performer] does not dispel your gloomy complaint, it must be desperate indeed."

The reply of the patient is worthy the attention of those who frequent such places in search of happiness, and it shows the utter emptiness and insufficiency of earthly pleasures.

"Alas, sir," said the patient, "I am Carlini; and while I delight all Paris with mirth, and make them almost die with laughter, I myself am dying with melancholy and chagrin."

This may but illustrate your case, as you carry a heavy heart beneath a smiling look. I will tell you the trouble. I will interpret yourself to yourself. You want Jesus of Nazareth! Have you noticed the meadow-vine in summer, creeping, creeping along on the ground; feeling its way after something; washed perhaps by the torrent, and lying prone with leaves and tendrils and flowers all soiled with mud; or, perhaps, twining its way up some stump or stake, and then turning its ends backward into itself, until it is a knotted, shapeless clump, with arms twisted and twined and tangled into each other? What is it after, and why this disorder? It wants something to lean upon, and lift itself upon. It is unknowingly searching, feeling its way, for some friendly tree up which it may climb, and around which it may rest and steady its expanding parts, blooming into thrifty leaves and flowers.

Image of your uneasy, unharmonious, unlovely, spiritual nature! It must love. It is putting out the arms of its affections and searching after something, you know not what. But that blind, unguided search is after Christ. It is feeling after him, if haply it might find him, though he may be not far from any one of us. This tells you what the matter is with you. The matter is your *soul* is hungry; it is starving; it is pining for the bread of heaven, for the absent Jesus, just like a little girl I saw one day in a beautiful home. Friends she had, playthings, attentions. But there was a look of sadness in her lustrous eye and upon her thin cheek. I knew the trouble: she was pining for her *dead mother*. And so are you for the absent Jesus, though, as in her case, the cause you may not be aware of.

Let your own felt need of happiness, then, your acknowledged lack of substantial, satisfying enjoyment, impel you to accept the Christ of the gospel.

What a motive should be your deliverance from the power and curse of sin! Whether you search God's word or your own heart, you must hear sounding in your ears, "Thou art weighed in the balance and art found wanting." It is but sober truth to say that your sins are more in number than the hairs of your head. And the question arises, How are you to get rid of these sins and escape their penalty? Get rid of them yourself, you cannot. Carry them into heaven, and they would change that place into hell. Christ alone takes away the sins of men; and for this you might well exclaim:

> "I need thee, precious Jesus,
>   For I am full of sin;
> My soul is dark and guilty,
>   My heart is dead within;
> I need the cleansing fountain,
>   Where I can always flee,
> The blood of Christ most precious,
>   The sinner's perfect plea."

Only one thing is possible to be done; it is to go to Jesus and obtain peace and pardon. Jesus gives both; he pardons the penitent, and he takes away the poison of sin. If you try to over-master and exterminate it, getting peace thus, you will find it a vain struggle. "Oh my sin, my sin!" cried Luther. "It is in vain I make promises to God; sin is always too strong for me." And that will be your experience. At a later period, when Luther had found out the secret of peace notwithstanding guilt, he says, "The devil came to me and said, 'Martin Luther, you are a great sinner and you will be damned!' 'Stop! stop!' said I, 'one thing at a time; I am a great sinner, it is true, though you have no right to tell me of it. I confess it;

what next?' 'Therefore you will be damned!' 'That is not good reasoning. It is true I am a great sinner, but it is written, "Jesus Christ came to save sinners," therefore I shall be saved. Now go your way!' So I cut the devil off with his own sword, and he went away mourning because he could not cast me down by calling me a sinner."

> "If all the sins which men have done,
>   In thought or will, in word or deed,
>   Since worlds were made or time begun,
>   Were laid on one poor sinner's head,
>   The stream of Jesus' precious blood
>   Could wash away the dreadful load."

Of old, church edifices were considered to be sanctuaries in which criminals might hide themselves, and so escape. See a transgressor rushing toward the church, the guards pursuing him with their drawn swords, athirst for his blood. They chase him even to the church door. But he rushes up the steps, and just as they are about to overtake him and hew him to pieces, out comes the bishop, and holding up the crucifix, cries, "Back, back! stain not the precincts of God's house with blood! stand back!" and the guards at once respect the emblem and stand back, while the poor fugitive hides himself behind the robes of the priest. "It is even so," says one using this figure, "with Christ. The guilty sinner flies to the cross—flies straight away to Jesus; and though Justice pursues him, Christ lifts up his wounded hands and cries to Justice, 'Stand back! stand back! I shelter this sinner, in the secret place of my tabernacle do I hide him; I will not suffer him to perish, for he has fled for refuge to me!'"

Do you not see in this your need of Jesus? And is it not simply because you have not had recourse to Christ that your sins are vexing you and your conscience is ill at ease?

In a certain hospital in the army a soldier had crawled with his crutch to the bedside of a comrade, anxious to know how it fared with one who had stood shoulder to shoulder with him in more than one affray.

"Well, how are you to-day?" inquired the visitor.

"I cannot say 'All's well,'" he replied, "either outwardly or inwardly; but the chaplain was here yesterday, and I told him I was miserable. I told him that I had tried pleasure, drink, everything, and that now my wretched mind was harder to bear than my wounds. What do you think he said? In the most solemn and earnest manner he said, 'Try Christ.' All night long those two words have been in my ears, 'Try Christ! Try Christ!'"

Ah, *you* would try him, sin-sick soul, if you knew how rich a benison he would bring!

It ought to be added, in speaking of sin, that to the young there is an argument for seeking Christ in the sinful practices from which one is kept by early piety. A little boy, whose father desired to see him a good child, was told one day that a nail would be driven into a post whenever he should do an act that was wrong, and when he should do a good deed he might pull one out. The little fellow tried to be good; and though there were a number of nails driven into the post, after a little while not one remained. Was Benny happy when he saw the last nail disappear from the post? His father was greatly pleased, and was congratulating his son, when he was surprised to see that he was weeping. And very touching was the remark he made:

"Ah, the nails are all gone, but the *marks are there still!*"

Is it not much if we have sought Jesus early and so escaped the marks of sin?

Before passing, then, to another consideration, will you not, my dear reader, pause a moment, and clasping the hands and lifting up the eyes and thoughts to heaven, repeat these beautiful lines, and do just what they declare?—

> "I lay my sin on Jesus,
>   The spotless Lamb of God;
> He bears them all, and frees us
>   From the accursed load.
>
> "I bring my guilt to Jesus,
>   To wash my crimson stains
> White in his blood most precious,
>   Till not a stain remains."

And what of *sorrows?* If free from them now you will not always be, "for man is born to trouble as the sparks fly upward." Rightly spake old Augustine: "God had one Son without sin, but he never had a son without sorrow." And what will you do when sorrows come? when sickness consumes the strength? when bereavement robs you of your jewels? when adversity frowns upon you at every step? Here again, if you apprehended your want, you would say:

> "I need thee, blessed Jesus—
> I need a friend like thee;
> A friend to soothe and pity,
> A friend to care for me.
>
> "I need the heart of Jesus
> To feel each anxious care,
> To tell my every trial
> And all my sorrows share."

We read in Gotthold's emblems that of an evening one of a company of friends despatched a servant to his house for a lute, and on being brought to the apartment it had lost tune, as usually happens to these instruments when exposed to the changes of the atmosphere.

While the owner was tightening the strings, Gotthold, who was present, thought within himself, What is sweeter than a well-toned lute, and what more delightful than a faithful friend who can cheer us in sorrow with wise and affectionate discourse? Nothing, however, is sooner untuned than a lute, and nothing is more fickle than a human friend. The tone of the one changes with the weather, that of the other with fortune. With a clear sky and a bright sun and a gentle breeze you will have friends in plenty, but let fortune frown and the firmament be overcast, and then your friends will prove like the strings of the lute, of which you will tighten ten before you will find one which will bear the tension or keep the pitch. It is painful to admit it, but there is a great deal of truth in this strong comparison.

Here is another emblem from the same source: "So long as there is blossom on the trees, and honey in the blossom, the bees will frequent them in crowds and fill the place with music; but when the blossom is over and the honey is gone, the bees too will all disappear. The same happens in the world with men. In the abode of fortune and pleasure friends will be found in plenty; but when fortune flies, they fly along with it. For this reason let good men be advised to fly to Christ crucified, who never forsakes, in their distress, those who truly seek him."

Besides this, earthly friends may be too far away to be of help to us, or they may die and leave us bereaved. But Jesus is always within hearing, always within reach—a friend that sticketh closer than a brother. He is the friend of the friendless; and "when my father and my mother forsake me, then the Lord will take me up." As then you will surely need comfort and strength in sore earthly trials, come by faith to the crucified One; ay, to the crucified One, in whom alone true comfort is found.

> "Is it not strange the darkest hour
> That ever dawned on sinful earth
> Should touch the heart with softer power
> For comfort than an angel's mirth?—
> That to the cross the mourner's eye should turn,
> Sooner than where the stars of Bethlehem burn?"

I have not yet spoken of the "last of earth"— of that moment when all earthly helpers fail. A little girl who was sick and near death said to her father one day,

"Father, it looks all dark in the grave. You must go with me into the grave; I can't go alone."

The father was so overcome that he left the room. She then appealed to her mother in the same words, who told her that neither father nor mother could do this. After a while she turned toward the wall and prayed, and then cheerfully said,

"I don't want you to go into the grave with me now, for I asked Jesus to go with me, and he says he will."

The kindest earthly friend could go no farther

than the place where the feet touch the waters of the river of death; but this friend says, "When thou passeth through the waters, I will be with you; and through the rivers, they shall not overflow you."

Contrast the sinner's death with that of the righteous. In the one case, the poor soul is encompassed on all sides with fear; bowed down by the insupportable burden of guilt; a conscience which is as a burning brand within the soul, set on fire by the anticipation of hell torments; dreading to depart, yet feeling that he must depart in a few moments more to the bar of divine justice, and thence to the abyss of unutterable torments.

The Hon. F. Newport, who had received a religious education, but turned infidel, said, in his last sickness, looking at the fire in his chamber, "Oh that I was to lie and broil upon that fire for a hundred thousand years to purchase the favor of God and be reconciled to him again! But it is a fruitless, vain wish. Millions of millions of years will bring me no nearer the end of my tortures than one poor hour. Oh, eternity! eternity! Who can properly paraphase upon the words 'for ever and ever'?"

"It is a fearful thing to die
 The death of a sinner's agony—
 A prayerless heart—no voice to plead—
 Thick darkness, and no hand to lead;
 To see beyond the open grave
 No star of hope—no arm to save—
 No ear for his despairing cry—
 It is a fearful thing to die."

But see how a Christian departs. A pious youth, dying in extreme bodily anguish, said to a friend standing by, "I would not exchange my place for that of a prince." President Edwards, when he came to die, after bidding his relations good-bye, said, "Now, where is Jesus of Nazareth, my true and never-failing friend?" So saying, he fell asleep. A good man, ready to depart, once said, "Methinks I stand, as it were, one foot in heaven and one on earth. Methinks I hear the melody of heaven, and by faith I see the angels waiting to carry my soul to the bosom of Jesus, and I shall be for ever with the Lord in glory. Who can choose but rejoice in all this?"

A soldier wounded in one of the battles of the late war was being carried from the field. He felt that his wound was mortal, that life was quickly ebbing away, and he said to his comrades who were carrying him,

"Put me down; do not take the trouble to carry me any farther; I am dying."

They then put him down and returned to the field. A few moments after, an officer saw the man weltering in his blood, and asked him if he could do anything for him.

"Nothing, thank you."

"Shall I get you a little water?" said the kind-hearted officer.

"No, thank you; I am dying."

"Is there nothing I can do for you? Shall I write to your friends?"

"I have no friends you can write to. But there is one thing for which I would be much obliged: in my knapsack you will find a Testament; will you open it at the fourteenth of John, and near the end of the chapter you will find a verse that begins with 'Peace.' Will you read it?"

The officer did so, and read the words: "Peace I leave with you, my peace I give unto you, not as the world giveth, give I unto you. Let not your heart be troubled, neither let it be afraid."

"Thank you, sir," said the dying man; "I have that peace, I am going to that Saviour,

God is with me, I want no more;" and he instantly expired.

Is it nothing to you, my dear friend, whether you do or do not thus die with heavenly support, and in the assurance of heavenly glory? Oh, embrace Christ; and then, whether called away in youth or age, yours shall be the departure of one concerning whom it was written:

> "No horror pales his lips nor rolls his eye,
> No dreadful doubt nor dreamy terrors start
> The hope Religion pillows on his heart,
> When, with a dying hand, he waves adieu
> To all who love so well, and weep so true.
> Calm as an infant to the mother's breast
> Turns fondly longing for its wonted rest,
> He pants to be where kindred spirits stay,
> Turns to his God, and breathes his soul away."

Take one more step. After death is the judgment; and here again see your need of Christ. Have you read of the ancient Roman who offended his sovereign and was forbidden his presence on pain of death? But it so occurred that he *must* see the emperor. There was no dispensing with it. How was it to be done? He hit upon this device. He lingered about the grounds of the palace and watched his opportunity, until he one day took up the little royal boy playing near by, and whose confidence he had gained, and with him in his arms he marched straight into the emperor's presence, saying, "Strike if you can! strike if you can!" Of course the monarch could not strike; he would have smitten his own flesh. So do as toward that offended God into whose presence you must come. This do with that SON of his love. Kiss the Son. Cease your neglect and abuse of him. By faith clasp him in your arms. Present him to God, and every day as you enter his presence in prayer ask for his sake admittance and acceptance. Live, putting him forward as your only plea and your only hope, and die clasping him to your breast; and go up there to meet a holy God face to face, humbly and yet boldly saying, "Thou canst not strike me now. It is thy Son. I make mention of thy righteousness, that which thou hast directed me to bring, even of thine only;" and like the old Roman, you are safe.

Can anything be plainer, then, than the truth of the proposition with which we set out, that we have deep soul-wants, spiritual necessities? And furthermore, is anything plainer than that Jesus Christ is the one great all-comprehensive good which the soul needs?—which *your* soul needs?

Shall this matter receive your serious and earnest attention? I know that pleasure presents to the young a gilded cup, and seriousness is distasteful. But I also know the deceptive and destructive nature of too much of that which the world calls pleasure, and that "he buys honey too dear who licks it from thorns."

Besides, there is a great truth in what Cardinal Richelieu said: "The soul is a serious thing, and it must be either sad here or be sad hereafter." We live amidst serious and earnest things, forget it as we may. Time is earnest, rushing us through life. Satan is earnest, working for our ruin. Death is earnest, cutting down our fellows on the right and the left. God is earnest, calling out, "Why will ye die?" It is madness, then, to give the soul no serious attention. We ought to feel like Myrogenes, who, when great gifts were sent unto him, sent them all back again, saying, "I only desire one thing at your master's hand, to pray for me that I may be saved for eternity." This was wisdom.

If serious feelings are now yours, I entreat of you do not suppress or smother them. Many a person's experience is drawn out in the remark of a young man who said, "When I was seventeen, I began to feel deeply at times, and this continued for two or three years, but I determined to put it off until I should be settled in life. After I was married, I reflected that the time had come when I had promised to attend to religion; but I had bought this farm, and I thought it would not suit me to become religious till it was paid for, as some time would have to be devoted to attend church, and also some expense. I then resolved to put it off ten years; but when the ten years came round, I thought no more about it." Oh, beware of such a result!

Nor mistake as to how you are to secure to yourself the conscious love and help of this Jesus. It is not by your good works, nor by vows and self-afflictions and painful struggles after righteousness, but by accepting Christ's work and deservings and sacrifice in your behalf and building thereon your hope. One word determines whether you are a true Christian— Christ. Have you taken hold of him? Do you cling to him? Do you make everything of him?

"There is a great difference between your religion and mine," said a Christian lady to one in whose spiritual condition she was interested. "Your religion has only two letters in it, and mine has four."

"What do you mean," said he, "by two letters and four?"

"Why, your religion," said the lady, "is d-o, do, whereas mine is d-o-n-e, done."

This was all that passed. But her words did their work in the soul of her friend. The entire current of his thoughts was changed. *Do* is one thing; *done* is quite another. The former is legalism; the latter is Christianity. It was a novel and very appropriate way of putting the gospel, but it was just the mode for a legalist, and the Spirit of God used it in the conversion of this man. When next he met his friend, he said to her,

"Now I can say, with you, that my religion is d-o-n-e, done."

He had learned to fling aside his deadly doings and to rest in the finished work of Christ alone. Perhaps this little incident is apposite to your case. Be sure your religion is in four letters—not "do," but "done."

"Betake thee to thy Christ, then, and repose
  Thyself in all extremities on those
    His everlasting arms,
Wherewith he girds the heavens, and upholds
The pillars of the earth, and safely folds
    His faithful flock from harms.
Cleave close to him by faith, and let the bands
Of love tie thee in thy Redeemer's hands."

VII.

NOW.

Ah! could we feel the weight of *now*,
    We should not wait with longing eyes,
And hope to do some noble work
    On morrows that may never rise.
Then help us, Lord, to know the way,
    To bear the toil, to meet the strife—
To thread each day a flawless gem
    Upon the silver cord of life."

"WILL my case be called in court to-day?" asked a client of his lawyer, with the greatest eagerness, having heard that it might be so.

"It is possible, sir," was the answer.

"Then are you sure that nothing is left undone? Do make a sure thing of it at once; for if the case goes against me, I am a ruined man." And he added, with yet more intense earnestness of look and expression, "I tell you, sir, there must be no *perhaps* here."

All this was natural enough in worldly concerns, and everybody would commend it as wise. But when it comes to soul-interests, we see men acting differently. They know the peril of delay—they admit the danger of it; but still they take the risk. Since their case before the great Judge may not be called to-day, they take advantage of the uncertainty,

> "And on this perhaps,
> This peradventure, infamous for lies,
> As on a rock of adamant, they build
> Their mountain hopes."

Of all Satan's devices he plies none with such dexterity as this. It is likely that more souls are ruined by the expectation of future repentance than by all things else put together. The way to perdition most surely is strewn with good intentions. Every one means to repent—expects to do it; but not now.

> "Thus at life's latest eve, we find in store
> One disappointment more, to crown the rest—
> The disappointment of a promised hour."

Against this fatal tendency of mankind the

merciful Father above lifts up his loud and loving remonstrance, saying, "Why will ye die?" "To-day, if ye will hear my voice!" "Behold, now is the accepted time—the time I accept—behold, now is the day of salvation."

How many facts and considerations go to emphasize this heavenly expostulation! That holy and earnest preacher, Richard Baxter, has enumerated and dwelt upon fifty reasons for immediate repentance. One would scarcely think that so many good reasons could be found, yet it is impossible to place the finger upon one of them and say it is not valid. Here they are in a minute and condensed form:

1. Consider to whom you are to turn—God.
2. To what you are to turn—holiness.
3. From what you are to turn—sin.
4. Delaying shows you would never part with sin if you might have your own will.
5. What a case you are in while thus delaying!
6. Delaying gives advantage to the tempter.
7. It abuses Christ and the Holy Ghost, who may leave you.
8. What is it you stay for?
9. The longer you stay, the harder the work will be.

10. Sin gets victory daily by your delay.

11. Age has inconveniences, youth advantages, therefore it is folly to delay.

12. More advantage than former ages or other nations.

13. Delaying runs a hazard; life is uncertain; grace is uncertain.

14. It increases your sin.

15. It increases God's anger against you.

16. It may damn the soul and body forever.

17. Time lost by delays is an inconceivable loss.

18. God has given no time to spare.

19. The greatness of the work to be done.

20. Many perish and few turn who willfully delay.

21. If turning be necessary, the sooner the better.

22. If you will not, you are without excuse.

23. Consider how long you have stayed already.

24. If you have hopes of salvation, is it ingenuous to continue in sin?

25. If you were sure of salvation, you will still suffer loss by delay.

26. How many stay for you while you delay! God the Father, Son, and Spirit, angels, ministers, and godly persons.

27. Christ did not delay to die.

28. God did not delay to do you good.

29. When you are to receive any outward deliverance, the sooner, then, you think, the better.

30. Your worldly delights are engaged in without delay.

31. Worldly business you delay not.

32. You delay not to receive gifts.

33. You should wait for God rather than he wait for you.

34. You will not delay helping others and you will not help yourself.

35. You deal worse with God than with the devil, for you delay not to do his will.

36. Speedy turning can do no harm and will never cause repentance.

37. It will grieve you much, if you do ever turn, that you turned no sooner.

38. Has God not a right to appoint the time? and he says, "To-day."

39. Dare you say you know better than God when to turn?

40. Quick coming makes you the more welcome.

41. Do with God as you would others should do to you.

42. Delay is a denial.

43. God does not stay for all as for you.

44. God will not always patiently wait.

45. Delays weary God's ministers.

46. Unspeakable loss you suffer while you delay.

47. You are doing what must be undone or you are undone.

48. Your conversion will be more grievous, more painful.

49. Delays are contrary to the nature of the work and the soul.

50. If you slumber, your damnation slumbereth not.

Now, seize upon any one of these motives, and perhaps yet others might be mentioned, and let the mind penetrate it, and one cannot fail to be convinced that "now" is indeed "the accepted time." Which of all has not force in it? Sweep over the whole of them, and say if this one or that were not alone a sufficient reason. Strike into the middle of the list, or begin at the top or the bottom, where do you find an exception?

If you classify this summary of reasons, you will find that each relates to one of several points which I specify.

1. Repentance should be immediate, because of the Being to whom we are to turn—that is, God. Is he not your Maker and Lord, whom you ought to serve? And has he not a right to appoint the time for obedience, when he says "to-day"? Is he not your Father, and Friend, and Benefactor? What favors he has shown! How rich and unremitted his benefits! Verily, "God did not delay to do you good;" and should not his goodness be appreciated and acknowledged by a loving heart and an obedient life? You treat no other friend so ill. You insult God's wisdom by seeming to say that you know better when to turn than he does. You despise his authority by treating with contempt his will. As Baxter says, "You deal worse with God than with the devil, for you delay not to do his will." What a thought! And yet upon consideration, you will admit the remark is just. And you trifle with the Divine long-suffering and goodness, which ought to have led you to repent-

ance. You should be ready and anxious to please and obey God, instead of thus compelling him to wait for your obedience.

You cannot have thought of the patience of that Father in waiting so long for you to repent.

> "God calling yet! shall I not rise?
> Can I his loving voice despise,
> And basely his kind care repay?
> He calls me still; can I delay?"

You cannot have thought of the love of Christ, for he did not delay even to die for you.

> "On wings of love the Saviour flew
> To raise you from the ground,
> And made the richest of his blood
> A balm for every wound."

And as to the Spirit, touched, I trust, by the thought of how you have grieved and resisted him, you must be ready to exclaim,

> "Stay, thou insulted Spirit, stay!
> Though I have done thee such despite,
> Cast not a sinner quite away,
> Nor take thine everlasting flight."

God-wise, then, what arguments are there for immediate repentance!

2. Then should not the change proposed be a powerful argument? It is from a state of con-

demnation to a state of justification. It is from a state of sinfulness to a state of holiness. Can you love sin? Is it not that dreadful, damning thing that God hates, the source of all our woes? But you add to sin by every hour's delay, and "show that you would never part with it if you might have your own will."

3. Then think of the increased difficulty of repentance by this delay. It is hard enough now for you to break away from the world. But sin is daily getting fresh victories over you, and binding you with stronger and tighter cords, so that "the longer you stay, the harder the work of reform will be."

4. Think, too, of the littleness of time and the exceeding greatness of its value. Have you any time to spare? But all is lost time till you repent, and is not this an inconceivable loss?

5. Then who can estimate the damage and the risk of delay? "Speedy turning," says Baxter, "can do no harm and will never cause repentance, but it will grieve you much, if you do ever turn, that you turned no sooner." How true! With each of those few who became Christians late in life, is it not a constant regret that sin was served so long? What a loss of

comfort, of peace of mind, and of opportunities to bless the world during a whole lifetime! Then how uncertain is life, upon which you hang your expectations of future repentance, increasing still more the risk!

> "Remember, life is but a shadow—
> Its date the intermediate breath we draw.
> Ten thousand accidents in ambush lie
> To crush the frail and fickle tenement,
> Which, like the brittle hour-glass measuring time,
> Is often broke ere half its sands are run."

Will you venture all on so frail a thing as life?

6. Consider, too, the nature of the excuses which you frame. How unfair and meanly unworthy to say, "I can repent later in life, and therefore I will put it off; I will live till the end comes, and then seek God"! A dying man, when urged to give himself to Christ, said, "No, I will not offer to Christ so mean a thing as the fag-end of my life." In his view a high sense of honor would not admit of such a thing. The blessed Saviour would not have refused thus to receive one at the eleventh hour; but is it manly to think of giving the best of our being to the love and service of self and sin, and then to bring the spent and worn-out energies and affections and

offer them to God? Is it honorable thus to cheat God of all we can, and then bring him the rest?

Then, too, how inconsistent is this excusing one's self from attention to religion! Surely "it is contrary to the work and the soul." You say, "Important things first," yet what is so important as preparation for death and heaven? and what is so deserving of attention as the soul? Was there ever such inconsistency?

How unreasonable too! Since the Father, Son, and Holy Spirit, and angels, and ministers, and godly persons, are concerned for your soul, is there not ground for this solicitude? and should you not be concerned for yourself? Moreover, you are eager to accept any outward deliverance, but will not permit the deliverance of your soul from the lowest hell. You gladly receive worldly gifts, but the inconceivably more valuable spiritual gifts you despise. At the same time the delights and the business of every-day life are entered into with alacrity, while you are slow to seek the kingdom of God, to the possession of which is added all conceivable good for this world and the next, according to God's own promise. Could anything be more ignoble, inconsistent, and unreasonable than this excusing yourself from immediate attention to the things of salvation?

7. Another important consideration is this: You have now peculiar advantages for turning to God. Very few have enjoyed, or do enjoy, advantages and opportunities such as yours, and you will not enjoy them a little hence as you do now. The time may come when you will sigh for privileges such as you have to-day.

Then, too, your years are passing, and maturity is approaching, which renders repentance still less likely. "Age has inconveniences and youth advantages, therefore it is folly to delay." Ask those in mature life if it is not so. They will tell how care presses, and responsibility increases, and the habits become confirmed, and there is less opportunity and less disposition to repent. Consult, too, the language of facts.

Nowhere has the writer met with such a forcible exhibition, such an appalling demonstration, of the fallacy and danger of this deceitful expectation which sinners so commonly cherish, as in a sermon by the late Dr. Spencer of Brooklyn. An accurate examination into the ages at which believers began Christ's service shows that the probability of conversion diminishes rapidly as the years roll on. This is his calculation: Make up a congregation of a thousand Christians. Divide them into five classes, according to the ages at which they became Christians. Place in the first class all those converted under twenty years of age; in the second class, all those converted between twenty and thirty; in the third class, all those converted between thirty and forty; in the fourth class, all those converted between forty and fifty; in the fifth class, all those converted between fifty and sixty. Then count each of the five classes separately. Of your thousand Christians there were hopefully converted—

>   Under 20 years of age............................ 548
>   Between 20 and 30 years of age.............. 337
>   Between 30 and 40 " " " 86
>   Between 40 and 50 " " " 15
>   Between 50 and 60 " " " 3

Here are your five classes; and if you will have a sixth class, and can call it a class, here it is:

>   Between 60 and 70 years of age.................. 1

Just one out of a thousand Christians converted over sixty years old. What a lesson on delay! What an awful lesson!

"I once made an examination of this sort," says Dr. Spencer, "in respect to two hundred and fifty-three converts to Christ who came under my observation at a particular period. Of this two hundred and fifty-three there were converted—

Under 20 years of age..............................	138
Between 20 and 30 years of age................	85
Between 30 and 40 " " "	22
Between 40 and 50 " " "	4
Between 50 and 60 " " "	3
Between 60 and 70 " " "	1

Beyond seventy, not one. How rapidly are cut off the hopes of the delaying as they continue on in life, making darker and darker the prospect as they are nearing the tomb! Let the sinner delay till he is twenty years old, and he has lost more than half the probability of salvation he had at twelve. Let him delay till he is thirty years old and he has lost three-fourths of the probability of salvation which he had at twenty. Let him delay till he has reached forty years, and only twenty-nine probabilities out of a thousand remain to him. Let him delay till he has reached fifty years, and beyond fifty there remain to him only fourteen out of a thousand.

We may strictly say that, as an unconverted man treads on into the vale of years, scarcely a single ray of hope remains to him. His prospect of conversion diminishes much faster than does his life. What an argument for repentance now!

8. Remember this, too, that delay is denial. A good resolve to be religious to-morrow is simply a bad resolve to be wicked to-day. Putting off is accounted by God as refusing. It *is* refusing; and this leads to a final point, viz.:

9. God may not continue patiently to wait. Putting off penitence is not putting off perdition. "If you slumber, your damnation slumbereth not." You are not repenting now; therefore you are sinning now, and therefore God is angry with you now. All his attributes are arrayed against you. His justice, wisdom, truth, and love unite in condemning you. His omnipresence pursues you, and his omnipotence is ready to punish you this very instant. Think, then, what you are doing—tampering with consuming fire!—bargaining with God, that if he will let you disobey somewhat longer, when you get ready you will repent!—haggling with him as to expected grace on the ground that he has not

struck you with his thunderbolt already! Oh, beware! There is such a Scripture as this: "Unto whom I sware in my wrath that they shall not enter into my rest." God does not always call for tardy comers. He sometimes heeds the request, "Go thy way."

> "There is a line by us unseen
> Which crosses every path—
> The hidden boundary between
> God's patience and his wrath."

Now, what will you do with this and these other arguments and persuasions to immediate repentance? I know you feel the force of them, and mean to be influenced by them; but tremble lest you practically say, "Not to-day, but to-morrow." Ah! take heed as to that treacherous, damning to-morrow. "To-morrow! Eloquent advocate! robed as a king's counsel, holding the devil's brief. The sermon's swift antidote, the preacher's most formidable respondent, never at a loss for a reply. To-morrow! Skillful fencer, warding off so dextrously the best aimed blows. To-morrow! Prompt physician, dulling the sense of pain by sweet but deadly narcotics, quieting the pangs of conscience, and closing up so comfortably the wounds of the sword of truth. To-morrow! Accomplished musician, soothing the soul to slumber by endless variations on a single string; delusive phantom, ever beckoning the traveler onward to destruction; courteous traitor, smiling assassin, Satan's chief recruiting-sergeant."

> "To-morrow, and to-morrow, and to-morrow,
> Creeps in this petty pace from day to day,
> To the last syllable of recorded time!
> And all our yesterdays have lighted fools
> The way to dusky death!"

Oh, I beg, I conjure you, to place against the devil's "to-morrow" God's "*to-day.*"

Just over the margin of a precipice, at Niagara Falls, where the mad current was boiling below, a young lady *would* pluck a flower shooting out from a cleft too far down to be reached. She leaned over the verge and caught a glimpse of the surging waters below the battlement of rocks, while fear for a moment darkened her excited mind. But there hung the lovely blossom upon which her heart was fixed, and she leaned in a delirium of intense desire and anticipation over the brink. Her arm was outstretched to grasp the beautiful thing, but the turf yielded to the pressure, and with a shriek she descended like a falling star to the rocky bottom and was borne away gasping in death. She only ventured a little too far! Did she mean to be killed? Oh no; but she ventured a little too far. And so may you, who sometimes hear the thunder of eternity's deep, and recoil a moment from the allurements of sin, yet venture on in pursuit of your fancied good until a despairing cry comes back from Jordan's waves, and your soul sinks into the horrors of the second death. Not expecting to be destroyed—that is why the rapid tide is sweeping such multitudes to perdition. All intend to repent. I tell you that for every soul in hell who determined to persevere in wickedness there are a thousand who did just what *you* are doing—promised to repent to-morrow!

Alexander, when one asked him how he had conquered the world, gave this answer, "By not delaying." Oh that I could bring you to a like course of action! Oh that, as the angel did with Lot when Sodom was to be destroyed, I could take you by the hand and effectually cry, "Escape for thy life; look not behind thee, neither stay thou in all the plain; escape to the mountain, lest thou be consumed!"

Drawing back, do you say, "I am too busy just now"? Then is it fit that you be told of the man who pleaded as a reason for not going to church that he lacked time and had to settle up his accounts on Sunday: the answer to which was, "The judgment-day will be spent, sir, in doing that same thing—settling up your accounts." So with you. You *will* find time to think of your soul's condition. "In the latter days ye shall consider it perfectly."

Do you say, "Just as good opportunities will occur again"? But every one understands that

> "We must take the current when it serves,
> Or we lose our ventures."

Opportunities present themselves and then pass by, and do not recur. The bank of the present is rich in opportunities, but when you next thrust your hand into the drawer you may find it empty. Your character and destiny may now be shaped like clay by the hands of the potter. Very soon it will pass into that state where it may be broken, but not reshaped.

> "The clay is moist and soft; oh, now make haste
> And form the pitcher, for the wheel turns fast."

To-day there is for you every promise, every

encouragement, every invitation, in God's book; but these are only for to-day. There is not one promise for to-morrow, and you perfectly well know that the irrevocable decree concerning you may be pronounced any moment, and that you may be weeping and wailing in despair before to-morrow.

> "Then stay the present instant,
> Imprint the marks of wisdom on its wings;
> 'Tis of more worth than kingdoms; far more precious
> Than all the crimson treasures of life's fountain.
> Oh, let it not elude thy grasp; but, like
> The good old patriarch upon record,
> Hold the fleet angel fast until he bless thee."

THE END.

www.ingramcontent.com/pod-product-compliance
Lightning Source LLC
Chambersburg PA
CBHW021823230426
43669CB00008B/847